Study Guide

for use with

Child Development

Tenth Edition

John W. Santrock
University of Texas at Dallas

Prepared by
Megan E. Bradley
Frostburg State University

Mc
Graw
Hill

Boston Burr Ridge, IL Dubuque, IA Madison, WI New York
San Francisco St. Louis Bangkok Bogotá Caracas Kuala Lumpur
Lisbon London Madrid Mexico City Milan Montreal New Delhi
Santiago Seoul Singapore Sydney Taipei Toronto

The McGraw·Hill Companies

Study Guide for use with
Child Development, Tenth Edition
John W. Santrock

Published by McGraw-Hill Higher Education, an imprint of The McGraw-Hill Companies, Inc., 1221 Avenue of the Americas, New York, NY 10020. Copyright © The McGraw-Hill Companies, Inc., 2004, 2001, 1998, 1996, 1994, 1992, 1989, 1987, 1982. All rights reserved.

This book is printed on acid-free paper.

1 2 3 4 5 6 7 8 9 0 QPD QPD 0 3

ISBN 0-07-282039-X

www.mhhe.com

CONTENTS

A Note to Students

Welcome to the study guide for *Child Development*, tenth edition, by John Santrock. The purpose of this guide is to facilitate your learning of the material in the textbook and in your class. In these next few pages, you will get an overview of the study guide as well as some learning tips that you can apply to this course or other courses.

How to Use this Study Guide.

Depending on your learning style, you might want to consult this study guide prior to your instructor reviewing the information in class, after a chapter has been read and discussed in class, and/or before an exam. The following features are designed to help you master course content and prepare for course exams:

Learning Goals. Your textbook includes learning goals at the beginning of each chapter. These goals highlight the main themes of the chapter and are reinforced by the "Review and Reflect" and "Reach Your Learning Goals" sections. Some students might be tempted to skip these sections while quickly reading through the material; but these sections are important to read and reflect upon as a way to increase your understanding of key concepts. In the study guide, each chapter begins with a review of the learning goals. Each goal is assigned a number and all of the subsequent questions list the corresponding goal or goals.

True or False Key Content Questions. These questions are intended to give you a review of various "facts" from the chapter. The statements typically represent the main idea of a given concept or the main finding of a research topic. They are a good review of important specific details from all of the learning goals. Remember: if any part of the statement is false, the whole statement is false.

Matching Key People Questions. Many times, individuals are responsible for making strides in an area of science. These questions ask you to match the important research finding or view to the corresponding person or people. They are another way to reinforce information from the learning goals. Sometimes it is more helpful to learn about a topic from the perspective of the person who originated the idea.

Multiple Choice Knowledge Questions. These questions give you good practice for taking a multiple-choice exam. The questions ask you to recall details and overall concepts from all of the learning goals. In conjunction with the True or False questions, they provide you with an extensive review of each chapter.

Critical Thinking Questions. These questions ask you to use your critical thinking skills in regards to one or more learning goals, and allow you to summarize information from the chapter.

Conceptual Questions. The aim of the True or False, Matching, Multiple Choice, and (to a degree) Critical Thinking questions is to help you retain information from the learning goals. The aim of the conceptual questions is to focus on the larger concepts in the chapter. Many of the conceptual questions ask you to apply your factual knowledge to a potential problem. Other conceptual questions ask you to use information to create a program aimed at enhancing children's development. Because you are applying your knowledge, you will achieve a deeper level of processing and understanding. Suggested answers are given in the answer key.

Applications. One of the best ways to learn about a new topic is to apply it your own life. The Santrock textbook and the Applications part of the study guide help make the learning goals more personal. Many of the Applications questions ask you to reflect on your own development and compare your experience to what is stated in the textbook. It is important to do a thorough comparison in order to retain the new information. Other questions from this section ask you to conduct observations of children, classrooms, or families. In this manner, you are applying your textbook knowledge to the "real world" and making comparisons between the two.

Answer key. At the end of each chapter is an answer key to the questions from that chapter. Each answer lists the corresponding textbook page number(s) where the correct answer can be found. If you get an incorrect answer, use the page reference to see how the information was presented in the chapter.

Study and Test Taking Tips.

Below are some tips and guidelines on studying and taking tests. You may use this information for this course or other courses:

Learning styles. One of the first things you want to do as a student is to figure out your learning style. You can divide learning styles into two categories: modality and information-processing. For modality, some students are *visual* learners, which means they learn best by having information presented to them visually. These students have a harder time retaining information if there are no visual aids. Other students are *auditory* learners who learn by listening to the information and may get distracted by visual presentations. Still other students are *tactile/experiential* learners who learn best when they can touch or experience concepts. They excel at laboratory courses or courses requiring an experiential component.

In regards to Information-Processing, some students process course material in a *detailed* manner. They typically take a lot of notes in class and are good at knowing factual information. But their weakness can be that they often do not understand the "big picture" or how concepts relate to one another. Other students process course material in a *conceptual* manner. These students take fewer notes and are good at knowing overall concepts. Their weakness can be that they miss important details.

Professors also have learning styles. Perhaps the main reason you are struggling in a course is that you have a different learning style than your professor. For example, if you process information in a conceptual manner but your professor is very detail-oriented, you are likely to feel frustrated in the classroom. Likewise, if you benefit from visuals but the professor only presents information verbally, you will likely have a hard time following the lecture.

Once you know your learning style, you can adapt how you approach classes to fit with your professor's style. If you need visuals, create them for yourself prior to class lecture by bringing an outline of the chapter with you. For auditory learners, you can read notes into a tape recorder and play the tape back to assist studying for a test. For experiential learners, you can recreate certain tasks from research studies or utilize the Applications section of this study guide. If you are detail-oriented, utilize the learning goals and outlines from the textbook and this study guide to highlight the "big picture." If you are conceptual, utilize the True or False, Matching, and Multiple Choice questions from this study guide to indicate what specific information you are missing. In addition, the Santrock textbook is designed to facilitate different learning styles. You can read about that in the Note to Students section of the textbook.

Form Study Groups. If you tended to study on your own in high school, consider getting into the habit of forming study groups in college. A study group can include two to six people (any more and you decrease the likelihood of getting work done). Try to include different learning styles in the group. For instance, a detail-oriented learner and a conceptual learner can become partners and assist with one another's area of weakness. You might consider taking advantage of the fact that many universities are setting up special dorms or floors in dorms of specific majors to facilitate study groups. You may also use online resources such as a virtual classroom to have study group discussions.

Dealing with Test Anxiety. Test anxiety is a situation-specific trait that involves anxious feelings and thoughts around the test-taking situation. It has two aspects: emotionality and worry. Emotionality is your body's reaction to the test, which typically manifests itself as accelerated heart rate, dry mouth, or a nervous stomach. The worry component is when one engages in "task irrelevant" thoughts that distract from the test questions. Two reasons for test anxiety are (a) poor study habits or (b) anxiety regarding tests. Here are some simple steps to take to reduce your test anxiety:

Step 1: Improve your study habits.

If your test anxiety is the result of poor studying, the best way to improve your situation is to improve your study habits. See the next section for information on how to accomplish this task.

<u>Step 2:</u> <u>Do a simple relaxation technique</u>.

Deal with the emotionality component of your text anxiety through a simple deep breathing exercise. Here is what you do:

- Take a normal breath in through your nose with your mouth closed.
- Exhale slowly with your mouth closed.
- Now, repeat this process but when you breathe, say the word RELAX to yourself like this:
  - inhale: "reeeee"
  - exhale: "lax"
- Practice this exercise several times a day, taking 10 to 15 breaths at each practice.

On the day of the exam, arrive to class early to begin your relaxation technique.

<u>Step 3:</u> <u>Cognitive Restructuring</u>.

Conquer the worry part of your test anxiety through a cognitive restructuring exercise. The first thing you want to do is to learn how to recognize when you are thinking "cognitive distortions". Typical irrelevant thoughts related to test anxiety include:

- What if I don't do well?
- I can't do this.
- This is too hard.
- I'm not smart enough.
- I bet everyone else knows the answers.
- Why is everyone else going so fast?
- I'm going to get the questions all wrong.

To eliminate these thoughts, imagine yourself in a typical testing situation, thinking one of the thoughts listed above. After thinking about it for about 20 seconds, shout STOP! (making sure you are in a place where you can yell!). What happened to the thought? It should have disappeared. Now repeat the process but this time yell STOP in your head, and imagine a large stop sign pushing out the negative thought. In its place a new thought emerges that reads: "I CAN DO THIS."

To summarize, in order to reduce your test anxiety that is not due to poor studying:

1) Do your deep breathing exercise: REEE - LAX
2) STOP any irrelevant thoughts.
3) Replace the negative thoughts with: "I CAN DO THIS".

Test Taking Tips. There are many ways to improve your chances of doing well on an exam. One suggestion is to **create a study space**. Make this space comfortable (but not too comfortable), spacious, and free of distractions such as the TV. Do whatever you need to do to make it an inviting place. Make sure you have good lighting and air flow. Take breaks as needed. Creating such a space makes it easier to motivate yourself to study for exams. You can also use this space to help you memorize information. For example, you can associate the objects on your desk with a list of words that you need to memorize. Then, during the test, you recall your desk to make it easier to recall the list of words.

A second suggestion is to **read a chapter once through completely**. If you read only part of a chapter, you will have a harder time learning the information without the broader context. Read the whole chapter either before you study various parts of it or after.

A third suggestion is to **take practice tests**. That is the main purpose of this study guide. Answer all of the questions in this guide, even if your professor informs you that you do not need to know a particular section. In this manner, you're completing your understanding of the broader context.

A forth suggestion is to **teach the material** to another person. This is one of the best ways to solidify your knowledge about concepts and remember information. You can teach the material in your study groups or to a helpful friend who does not mind learning about a topic from a different course.

A final suggestion is to **let the test help you**. In most circumstances, you want to answer the easy, short questions first. This will give you confidence and allow you to quickly recall details from your memory. Answer conceptual questions last because this information will be stored at a deeper level in your memory and can be more easily retrieved after answering other questions. Look for answers in other test questions. Sometimes a fact that you can't remember on one question will appear as part of another question. Sometimes you can remember different parts to an essay question by reading the multiple-choice questions.

Final thoughts.

As mentioned above, one of the best ways to learn and retain information is to apply it to your own life. It can be hard to do that in some college courses such as calculus. However, this course on child developmental psychology makes applying information to your own life easy. Not only will you learn about a new topic but you will learn about your own development. Child development is an interesting and exciting topic. I hope you enjoy this learning experience.

Good luck and have fun learning!
Megan E. Bradley, Ph.D.

SECTION 1: THE NATURE OF CHILD DEVELOPMENT
CHAPTER 1: INTRODUCTION

A.   *LEARNING GOALS*

Child Development-Yesterday and Today

LG 1: Discuss the Past and the Present in the Field of Child Development.

Developmental Processes and Periods

LG 2: Identify the Most Important Developmental Processes and Periods.

Developmental Issues .

LG 3: Describe Three Key Developmental Issues.

B. TRUE OR FALSE KEY CONTENT QUESTIONS

Why Study Children?

1. (T) F   One reason why it is important to study children and child development is to understand how children change as they grow up and the forces that contribute to this change. (LG 1)

Child Development—Yesterday and Today

2. (T) F   During the past century, the study of child development evolved from a philosophical perspective to a direct observation and experimentation perspective. (LG 1)

3. T (F)   The ultimate responsibility for the health and well-being of our children rests with physicians. (LG 1)

4. (T) F   Children who have been maltreated by their parents are more likely to be aggressive towards peers. (LG 1)

5. (T) F   Despite its size, the culture of a country influences the identity, learning, and social behavior of its members. (LG 1)

6. (T) F   Demographic trends indicate an increasing ethnic diversity in the United States. (LG 1)

7. T (F)   Ethnicity is a more powerful indicator of the type of home environment children experience than poverty. (LG 1)

Developmental Processes and Periods

8. (T) F   Biological, cognitive, and creative processes are interwoven as a child develops. (LG 2)

9. (T) F   Early childhood is a time when children focus on the fundamental skills of reading, writing, and arithmetic. (LG 2)

Developmental Issues

10. (T) F   The nature/nurture controversy is a debate about whether development is primarily influenced by maturation or by experience. (LG 3)

11. (T) F   The continuity of development view is that development involves gradual, cumulative change. (LG 3)

12. (T) F   The discontinuity of development view is that development involves distinct stages in the life span. (LG 3)

13. (T) F   The early-later experience issue focuses on when experiences determine a child's development. (LG 3)

14. T (F)   Most developmentalists recognize the wisdom of taking extreme positions on what influences development. (LG 3)

C. MATCHING KEY PEOPLE QUESTIONS

F 1. The president of *Children's Defense Fund* who advocates actively on the behalf of children. (LG 1) Edman

E 2. The individual who proposed an enlightened view of the nature of children and their rearing. (LG 1) Rousseau

H 3. The developmental researcher who devised the photographic dome to study children unobtrusively. (LG 1) Gesell

B 4. Researcher who observed the environmental and behavioral influence on children's behavior. (LG 1) Watson

G 5. Swiss psychologist famous for identifying cognitive stages from infancy through adolescence. (LG 1) Piget

C 6. This psychoanalyst stressed that a child's experience with parents in the first five years of life is an important determinant in later personality development. (LG 1) Freud

D 7. French psychologist who studied attention and memory in the early 1900s. (LG 1) Binet

A.   Kenneth Clark

B.   John Watson — 4

C.   Sigmund Freud — 6

D.   Alfred Binet

E.   Jean-Jacques Rousseau 1

F.   Marian Wright Edelman |

G.   Jean Piaget 5

H.   Arnold Gesell — 3 (photo)

I.   Jerome Kagan

J.   John Locke

K.   Philippe Aries

D. MULTIPLE CHOICE KNOWLEDGE QUESTIONS

1. (LG 1) Philippe Aries's review of art and publications during the Middle Ages led him to conclude that

    a. infancy was accepted as a distinctive period of life by Europeans as early as the Middle Ages.

    b. childhood was not recognized as a distinctive period by Europeans prior to the 1600s.

    c. adolescence was the focus of much early literature and art throughout the world.

    d. early literature recognized several distinct developmental periods.

 2. (LG 1) The current view of childhood assumes that

    a. children are similar to adults in most ways.

    b. children are best treated as young adults.

    c. childhood is basically a "waiting period."

    d. childhood is a unique period of growth and change.

 3. (LG 1) Baldwin's view of children highlighted

    a. development of intelligence tests.

    b. conscious thoughts.

    c. unconscious thoughts.

    d. peer relationships.

4. (LG 1) Which of the following is a concern for contemporary families?

    a. need for both parents to work

    b. increased importance of television

    c. increase in single parent homes

    d. both (a) and (c)

5. (LG 1) Research has demonstrated that one way to improve the education of our nation's children is to

    a. extend school days.

    b. emphasize more memorization.

    (c.) promote mentoring programs.

    d. promote summer school.

6. (LG 2) The period of development where children learn to become more self-sufficient and develop

school readiness skills is

    a. infancy.

    b. early childhood.

    c. middle and late childhood.

    d. adolescence.

7. (LG 3) Proponents of the nurture view would argue that

    a. the environment a person is raised in is the most important determinant of his or her longevity.

    b. genetics determine all behavior.

    c. how long an individual's parents lived is the best predictor of his or her longevity.

    d. both genetics and the environment an individual is raised in combine to determine longevity.

8. (LG 3) If the results of a study of cognitive development indicate that the change from concrete

thinking to abstract thinking occurs abruptly, which of the following views has been supported?

    a. continuity

    b. stability

    c. discontinuity

    d. dialectical

9. (LG 3) The question, "Will the shy child who never speaks turn into a quiet, shy adult or will the child become a sociable, talkative person?" is concerned with which developmental issue?

    a. maturation and experience

    b. continuity and discontinuity

    (c.) early and later experience

    d. nature and nurture

10. (LG 3) Most psychologists believe that development is due _interaction of nature/nurture_

    a. largely to nature.

    b. largely to nurture.

    c. to nature and nurture acting separately.

    (d) to an interaction of nature and nurture.

E. CRITICAL THINKING QUESTIONS

1. Explain why it is important to study children and child development. (LG 1) ✓

2. Define culture. How does cultural development influence a group of people? (LG 1)

3. Compare and contrast the early experience doctrine with the later experience doctrine of child development. Which doctrine would you advocate? Why? (LG 3)

4. How do prevention programs and competency training increase a child's resilience? (LG 1)

F. CONCEPTUAL QUESTIONS

1. Using the research results reported in Figure 1.3, how would you devise a prevention program for families aimed at decreasing the use of spanking as a form of discipline and increasing the number of books children own? (LG 1)

2. A seven-year-old child struggles at school in the areas of math and reading. How would each of the following perspectives view this child's difficulties? (LG 3)

    a. nature side of nature/nurture debate

    b. nurture side of nature/nurture debate

    c. early side of early-later experience issue

    d. later side of early-later experience issue

G. APPLICATIONS

Reflect upon and write about the personality and traits of you and your sibling(s), or siblings from another family. What similarities do the siblings have in common? What differences exist? How would you explain these similarities and differences from the perspective of the nature side of the nature/nurture debate? From the nurture side?

ANSWER KEY

B. TRUE OR FALSE KEY CONTENT QUESTIONS

1. T (6)
2. T (8)
3. F (10)
4. T (12)
5. T (12)
6. T (13)
7. F (14)
8. T (17)
9. F (18)
10. T (19)
11. T (20)
12. T (20)
13. T (20)
14. F (21)

C. MATCHING KEY PEOPLE QUESTIONS

1. F (15)
2. E (7)
3. H (9)
4. B (9)
5. G (9-10)
6. C (8-9)
7. D (8)

D. MULTIPLE CHOICE KNOWLEDGE QUESTIONS

1. b (7)
2. d (7)
3. b (9)
4. d (10)
5. c (12)
6. b (13)
7. a (19)
8. c (20)
9. c (20-21)
10. d (21)

E. CRITICAL THINKING QUESTIONS

1. (6–10)
   - Responsibility for children is a collective responsibility.
   - Childhood lays an important foundation for the adult years.
   - Childhood has distinct periods where children master skills.
   - Children need to be protected from the excesses of the adult world.

2. (12–14)
   - Culture refers to the behavior patterns, beliefs, and other products of a particular group of people that are passed on from generation to generation.
   - Cultural products are the result of the interaction between people and their environment.
   - A cultural group can be large (e.g., the United States) or small (e.g., African tribe).
   - A cultural group influences the social behavior of its members.

3. (20)
   - The early experience doctrine suggests that prime learning and cognitive development occur in the first few years of life. If the infant does not experience warm, nurturing care during these years, later development will be diminished.
   - The later experience doctrine suggests that entire life-span development is more important than a rigid identification to one period. Later sensitive care-giving is just as important as earlier sensitive care-giving.

4. (16)
   - The literature on resiliency indicates that a combination of individual, family, and extrafamilial factors improve resiliency in children. Successful prevention programs promote specific skill-building in children. Improving a child's competence in problem-solving, assertiveness, self-control, and decision-making can help reduce aggressive behavior and improve social interaction.

F. CONCEPTUAL QUESTIONS

1. Your prevention plan would focus on families who are living in poverty, regardless of ethnicity. (14)

2. Each view would emphasize a different explanation for the child's difficulty:
   a. Nature: child inherited academic difficulties
   b. Nurture: child's family does not promote education in the house
   c. Early: child's problems will continue because you cannot overcome early difficulties
   d. Later: child's problems can improve because children are malleable throughout development

   (19–21)

CHAPTER 2: THE SCIENCE OF CHILD DEVELOPMENT

A. LEARNING GOALS

Theories of Child Development

LG 1: Describe Theories of Development

Research in Child Development

LG 2: Explain How Research on Life-Development is Conducted.

Facing Up to Research Challenges

LG 3: Discuss Research Challenges in Child Development

B. TRUE OR FALSE KEY CONTENT QUESTIONS

Theories of Development

1. T (F)   Sigmund Freud's personality structure is characterized by id, ego, and shame. (LG 1)

2. (T) F   Erik Erikson's is based on eight stages of psychosocial development that confronts individuals with a crisis that must be addressed. (LG 1)

3. (T) F   Jean Piaget's four-stage cognitive development theory asserts that mental development is a continuous creation of increasingly complex forms. (LG 1)

4. T (F)   Lev Vygotsky's contribution to cognitive theory claims that cognitive skill development is separate from language development and sociocultural activities. (LG 1)

5. (T) F   The information-processing perspective emphasizes the learning of strategies. (LG 1)

6. (T) F   B. F. Skinner's operant conditioning is based on how consequences influence behavior. (LG 1)

7. (T) F   Social cognitive theorists believe that children acquire behaviors, thoughts, and feelings through observing others' behavior. (LG 1)

8. T (F)   Imprinting refers to the unique characteristic of an individual's fingerprints. (LG 1)

9. T (F)   One contribution of ethological theory is its attention to cognition. (LG 1)

10. (T) F   Ecological theory supports the view that multiple environments such as family, peer, and school give a more complete picture of an individual's development. (LG 1)

Research Methods in Child Development

11. T F   The goal of correlational research is to describe how strongly two events are related or associated. (LG 2)

12. T F   The goal of experimental research is to determine the cause of behavior through carefully controlled experiments. (LG 2)

13. T F   Longitudinal research involves studying the same individuals over a long period of time, usually several years or more. (LG 2)

14. T F   The abstract is the results of the data that appears at the end of a research journal article. (LG 2)

Facing Up to Research Challenges

15. T F   The code of ethics adopted by the American Psychological Association (APA) protects researchers from legal harassment from participants. (LG 3)

16. T F   Ethnic gloss is a positive addition to research on child development. (LG 3)

C. MATCHING KEY PEOPLE QUESTIONS

Frued/Erikson

_C_ 1. The psychoanalysist who emphasized the examination of symbolic meanings to understand development. (LG 1)

_L_ 2. The individual who argued that more children from ethnic minority backgrounds need to be included in research. (LG 3) *Pam Reid*

_D_ 3. The originator of an environmental, contextual theory of development that includes five environmental systems. (LG 1)

_K_ 4. One of the two individuals whose behavioral theory emphasizes the roles of behavior, cognition, and environment in development. (LG 1) ✓✓

_A_ 5. A psychoanalytic theorist who proposed that development entails eight psychosocial stages. (LG 1) *Eric Erikson*

_H_ 6. The Russian physiologist who developed the concept and procedure of classical conditioning. (LG 1) *Pavlov*

_I_ 7. The individual who proposed that attachment to a caregiver has important implications for one's life. (LG 1)

_G_ 8. The proponent of a cognitive theory of development that entails four qualitatively different *Piaget* stages. (LG 1)

A. Erik Erikson

B. Keith Stanovich

C. Sigmund Freud

D. Urie Bronfenbrenner

E. Lev Vygotsky

F. Konrad Lorenz

G. Jean Piaget

H. Ivan Pavlov

I. John Bowlby

J. B. F. Skinner

K. Albert Bandura

L. Pam Reid

D. MULTIPLE CHOICE KNOWLEDGE QUESTIONS

1. (LG 1) Developing a study schedule is a function of the *ego*

    a. id.

    b. ego.

    c. superego.

    d. ego-ideal.

2. (LG 1) Erik Erikson's theory emphasized

    a. repeated resolutions of unconscious conflicts about sexual energy.

    b. changes in children's thinking as they matured.

    c. success in confronting specific conflicts at particular ages in life.

    d. the influence of sensitive periods in the various stages of biological maturation.

3. (LG 1) When four-year-old Amadeus hears a concerto on the radio, he begins to move his hands up and down in a motion that resembles a person playing the piano. Amadeus's behavior exemplifies Piaget's

    a. sensorimotor stage.

    b. preoperational stage.

    c. concrete thinking stage.

    d. formal operational stage.

4. (LG 1) If you want to increase the number of times your spouse does the dishes, B. F. Skinner would tell you to

    a. yell at your spouse when he or she does not do the dishes.

    b. kiss your spouse when he or she does the dishes.

    c. leave the sink full of dishes until your spouse does them.

    d. ask your spouse nicely to do the dishes.

15

5. (LG 1) One of the strong points of behavior theory is its

   a. emphasis on the environment in explaining children's behavior.

   b. belief that cognitive processes are irrelevant for understanding development.

   c. emphasis on reducing children's behavior to fine-grained elements.

   d. emphasis on the role of information processing as a mediator between behavior and
   environment.

6. (LG 1) Barbara insists that to assure bonding she must be conscious and have an opportunity to see
   and hold her baby immediately after its delivery. Which of the following theories would agree with
   Barbara?

   a. ethological theory

   b. humanistic theory

   c. psychoanalytic theory

   d. learning theory

7. (LG 1) A major strength of ecological theory is its framework for explaining

   a. environmental influences on development.

   b. biological influences on development.

   c. cognitive development.

   d. affective processes in development.

8. (LG 2) How is a questionnaire study different from one that uses interviews?

   a. Questionnaires usually involve in-depth probing into the details of a person's life.

   b. Interviews may be carried out over the phone, while questionnaires are always completed with
   the researcher present.

   c. Questionnaires ask respondents to indicate their answers on paper instead of answering orally.

   d. Interviews are the preferred method for cross-cultural research.

9. (LG 2) Which of the following research techniques would be the best choice to investigate a child who is a chess prodigy?

    a. survey

    b. experiment

    c. standardized test

    (d.) case study

10. (LG 3) Florence Denmark highlighted what type of bias in research?

    a. overselection of males as participants

    (b.) unduly magnified gender differences

    c. underselection of minorities as participants

    d. ethnic gloss

E. CRITICAL THINKING QUESTIONS

1.   What are the strengths and weaknesses of these theories: psychoanalytic, cognitive, behavioral/social learning, ethological, and ecological? (LG 1)

2.   Compare and contrast research conducted in the laboratory with naturalistic observation. (LG 2)

3.   Why do researchers use random assignment in experimental research? (LG 2)

4.   Explain how gender bias may have influenced research on female achievement in math. (LG 1)

F. CONCEPTUAL QUESTIONS

1. Freud would reason that a typical five-year-old child is experiencing the resolution of the Oedipus complex as part of the phallic stage of psychosexual development. What would Erikson and Piaget say about what that same five-year-old child is experiencing in his or her life? (LG 1)

2. You are interested in researching children's activity levels and their overall physical health. Design an experiment to test your hypothesis that children who are active everyday are in good health, using one treatment group and one control group. (LG 2)

   a) Describe your research study and who will comprise your 2 groups.

   b) What is your independent and dependent variable?

   c) Revise your study to be a cross-sectional experimental design.

   d) How would you test the same hypothesis using a correlational design instead of an experiment? If your hypothesis were true, would it be a positive or negative correlation?

G. APPLICATIONS

Interview a developmental psychologist about their research on children (there is probably one in your school's psychology department). What ethical considerations do they face? Do they favor cross-sectional or longitudinal approaches? If you were to do research on children's development, what area would you choose?

ANSWER KEY

B. TRUE OR FALSE KEY CONTENT QUESTIONS

1. F (30)
2. T (31–32)
3. T (34)
4. F (35)
5. T (36)
6. T (37)
7. T (38)
8. F (39)
9. F (39)
10. T (40)
11. T (46)
12. T (47)
13. T (48–49)
14. F (50)
15. F (52)
16. F (55–57)

C. MATCHING KEY PEOPLE QUESTIONS

1. C (30)
2. L (31–32)
3. D (40)
4. K (37–38)
5. A (31–32)
6. H (37)
7. I (39)
8. G (33)

D. MULTIPLE CHOICE KNOWLEDGE QUESTIONS

1. b (30)
2. c (31–32)
3. b (34)
4. b (37
5. a (38)
6. a (39)
7. a (40)
8. c (45)
9. d (46)
10. b (54–55)

E. CRITICAL THINKING QUESTIONS

1. (33–41)

	Strengths	Weaknesses
psychoanalytic	early, unconscious experiences emphasized	cognition hardly emphasized
cognitive & environment emphasis	interaction, adaptation emphasized	little emphasis on information processing
behavioral/social learning	environment viewed as cause of behavior	little emphasis on cognition
ethological	biology viewed as cause of behavior	little emphasis on cognition
ecological	environmental systems & sociohistorical emphasis	little emphasis on cognition & biology

2. (44–45)
   - Laboratory studies allow researchers more control over the behavior of participants. This allows for more systematic observation. However, laboratory studies are criticized as being artificial. Naturalistic observation happens in real world settings, such as classrooms, homes, museums, malls, etc. It is very difficult to control for extraneous variables in such settings. Also, the unpredictability of interactions cannot be isolated.

3. (48)
   - Random assignment involves putting participants with similar attributes (age, family background, intelligence, socioeconomic factors, etc.) in experimental and control groups by chance alone. Random assignment greatly reduces the probability that the two groups will differ. This allows researchers to have more confidence about interpreting the effect or intervention given to the experimental group.

4. (54–56)
   - Effort needs to be made to make research equitable for both males and females.
   - In the past, research was often biased against females.

F. CONCEPTUAL QUESTIONS

1. Erikson would place the child in the initiative versus guilt stage and say that the child is dealing with developing a sense of responsibility and initiative while avoiding uncomfortable guilt and anxiety. Piaget would place the child in the preoperational stage and say that the child is able to symbolically represent his or her world through words, images, and drawings but still lacks the concept of *operations*. (30–35)

2. Your research study can be on any childhood age.
    a. The treatment group would be children who are active every day. Your control group would be children who are not active.
    b. The independent variable would be activity level (active vs. not active) and the dependent variable would be children's health.
    c. An example of a cross sectional design would be to test children in second, fourth, and sixth grades because you are testing children of different ages at the same time.
    d. To make it a correlational study, you could survey children on their level of activity and their overall health to see if they significantly relate. If your hypothesis were true, then you would get a positive correlation: As children's activity levels increase, their overall health increases/improves. (46–50)

SECTION 2: BIOLOGICAL PROCESSES, PHYSICAL DEVELOPMENT, AND PERCEPTUAL DEVELOPMENT

CHAPTER 3: BIOLOGICAL BEGINNINGS

A. LEARNING GOALS

The Evolutionary Perspective

LG 1: Discuss the Evolutionary Perspective.

Genetic Foundations

LG 2: Describe the Genetic Foundations of Development.

Reproduction Challenges and Choices

LG 3: Identify Some Important Reproduction Challenges and Choices.

Heredity-Environment Interaction

LG 4: Explain Heredity-Environment Interaction.

B. TRUE OR FALSE KEY CONTENT QUESTIONS

The Evolutionary Perspective

1. T F   Natural selection favors individuals that are best adapted to survive and

reproduce. (LG 1)

2. T F   Evolutionary psychology emphasizes the importance of adaptation, reproduction,

and "survival of the fittest" in explaining behavior. (LG 1)

Genetic Foundations

3. T F   The nucleus of each human cell contains 42 chromosomes, which come in 21 pairs, one

from each parent. (LG 2)

4. T F   Mitosis is the process by which cells divide into gametes for cell growth and

repair. (LG 2)

5. T F   Reproduction begins when a female gamete (ovum) is fertilized by a male gamete

(sperm) to produce a zygote. (LG 2)

6. T F   If one gene of a pair is dominant and one is recessive, the dominant gene overrides a

recessive gene. (LG 2)

7. T F   According to the reaction range, anyone can achieve high intelligence with the right kind

of stimulating environment. (LG 2)

8. T F   Canalization describes the study of hereditary influence on development. (LG 2)

9. T F   Fraternal twins develop from a single fertilized egg that splits into two genetically

identical replicas. (LG 2)

10. T F   The Human Genome Project is the construction of a map of each human gene. (LG 2)

11. T F   Results from the Human Genome Project indicate a one-to-one correspondence between

genes and behavior. (LG 2)

Reproductive Challenges and Choices

12. T   F   Chorionic villa sampling is a prenatal test during the last trimester to detect for birth

defects. (LG 3)

13. T   F   Zygote intrafallopian transfer is a process in which an egg and a sperm are combined in a

laboratory dish. (LG 3)

14. T   F   Researchers have found that adopted children and adolescents often show more

psychological and school-related problems than non-adopted children. (LG 3)

Heredity-Environment Interaction

15. T   F   Niche-picking refers to finding a niche or setting suited to one's compatibility, such as

attractive adolescents seeking out attractive peers. (LG 4)

16. T   F   Nonshared environmental experiences are likely to be the reason one sibling's

personality is different from another's. (LG 4)

C. MATCHING KEY PEOPLE QUESTIONS

___ 1. A behavior geneticist who believes that parental genotypes influence the environments that they provide for their offspring. (LG 2)

___ 2. The individual who proposed the principle of natural selection. (LG 1)

___ 3. Author of the book *The Dependent Gene*, which asserts that genes and the environment together influence our characteristics. (LG 2)

___ 4. The individual who directs the Minnesota Study of Twins Reared Apart Project. (LG 1)

___ 5. An evolutionary psychologist who believes that behavior needs input from psychological mechanisms. (LG 1)

___ 6. A behavior geneticist who believes that shared environments account for little of the variation in children's interests and personality. (LG 4)

___ 7. Author of the book *The Nature Assumption*, which asserts that an individual's genetic imprint is more important to development than the influence of parents. (LG 4)

A. Thomas Bouchard

B. Judith Harris

C. Charles Darwin

D. Robert Plomin

E. David Buss

F. David Moore

G. Jerome Kagan

H. Sandra Scarr

I. William Greenough

J. T. Berry Brazelton

D. MULTIPLE CHOICE KNOWLEDGE QUESTIONS

1. (LG 1) Evolutionary theory interprets gender differences in children's play as

    a. domain-specific modules.

    b. preparation for adulthood.

    c. adapting to current context.

    d. not adaptive in contemporary society.

2. (LG 2) The process of cell division in which each pair of chromosomes separates and joins a daughter cell is called

    a. reproduction.

    b. mitosis.

    c. meiosis.

    d. gametization.

3. (LG 2) Assume that the gene for green hair is dominant, whereas the gene for blue hair is recessive. Which of the following statements is most accurate?

    a. Parents with green hair can have a child with blue hair.

    b. Parents with blue hair can have a child with green hair.

    c. Parents with blue hair cannot have a child with blue hair.

    d. Parents with green hair cannot have a child with green hair.

4. (LG 2) A person's genetic heritage is his or her _____, whereas the expression of the genetic heritage is his or her _____.

    a. genotype; phenotype

    b. dominant character; recessive character

    c. phenotype; genotype

    d. recessive character; dominant character

27

5. (LG 2) A child who was raised in an abusive environment grows up with normal social and cognitive skills. This result is best explained by

    a. phenotype.

    b. canalization.

    c. DNA.

    d. polygenic inheritance.

6. (LG 2) In an adoption study, a psychologist compares the behavior of

    a. identical and fraternal twins.

    b. family members and randomly selected others.

    c. fraternal twins with each other.

    d. children living with adoptive parents and children living with biological parents.

7. (LG 3) A physician orders that an amniocentesis be performed to determine whether a woman's fetus is genetically normal. This procedure will involve

    a. taking a blood sample from the mother.

    b. drawing a sample of the fluid that surrounds a baby in the womb.

    c. taking a sample of the placenta between the eighth and eleventh week of pregnancy.

    d. taking a blood sample from the fetus.

8. (LG 3) *In vitro* fertilization is a possible solution to infertility that involves

    a. having sperm and egg unite outside of a woman's body.

    b. implanting a fertilized egg into a substitute mother's womb.

    c. enhancing the possibility of conception by taking fertility drugs.

    d. incubating a zygote outside of a woman's body.

9. (LG 4) Children who are highly active and athletic elicit adult encouragement to join sports teams. This describes an example of a/an _____/environment interaction.

    a. passive genotype

    b. active genotype

    c. niche-picking genotype

    d. evocative genotype

10. (LG 4) All three of the Brodsky children grew up in the same house, went to the same school, and observed their parents' dedication to charitable work. These expectations constitute the children's

    a. shared environmental influences.

    b. non-shared environmental influences.

    c. niche-picking experiences.

    d. heritability.

E. CRITICAL THINKING QUESTIONS

1. What are some psychological consequences for families receiving fertility treatments? (LG 3)

2. Explain why genotypes drive experience. (LG 2)

F. CONCEPTUAL QUESTIONS

1. Joan's family has a history of Fragile X Syndrome. She is pregnant with her first child, who is a boy. Using the sex-linked genetic principle and the polygenetic inheritance, how might you explain the risk that her child will be born with Fragile X Syndrome? If her son is born with this syndrome, could he achieve a high IQ if he is raised in a stimulating environment? (LG 2)

2. A married couple is having difficulty conceiving a child. What options are available for them? Include options related to fertility clinics and adoption. What are the pros and cons of each option? (LG 3)

G. APPLICATIONS

Contact the nearest fertility clinic in your area. What fertility options do they offer? What is the typical success rate of their services? What is the average cost of a procedure? Compare their answers to the information given in your textbook.

ANSWER KEY

B. TRUE OR FALSE KEY CONTENT QUESTIONS

1. T (67)
2. T (68)
3. F (70)
4. F (70)
5. T (71)
6. T (71)
7. F (73)
8. F (74)
9. F (74)
10. T (75)
11. F (75)
12. F (81)
13. F (82)
14. T (83)
15. T (85)
16. T (86)

C. MATCHING KEY PEOPLE QUESTIONS

1. H (73)
2. C (67)
3. F (75)
4. A (66)
5. E (68)
6. D (86)
7. B (86)

D. MULTIPLE CHOICE KNOWLEDGE QUESTIONS

1. b (68)
2. c (70)
3. a (71–72)
4. a (73)
5. b (74)
6. d (75)
7. b (81)
8. a (82)
9. d (85)
10. a (86)

E. CRITICAL THINKING QUESTIONS

1.   (83)
   - The increasing use of fertility drugs is producing greater numbers of multiple births. Multiple births increase the likelihood that the babies will have life-threatening problems, such as low birth weight. These medical risks also mean higher costs, which may not be paid by insurance companies. However, families begun by using reproductive technologies showed no differences in children's socioemotional development than families begun from natural conception.

2.   (73)
   - Genotypes are an individual's inherited environment that is related to genetic propensities. For example, a cooperative, attentive child evokes more instructional response from adults than an uncooperative, belligerent child. This is an example of evocative-genotype environmental correlation. In another example, attractive adolescents seek out attractive adolescent peers. This is an example of active-genotype environmental correlation.

F. CONCEPTUAL QUESTIONS

1. Fragile X Syndrome is an X-linked genetic disorder. Since she has family history of the syndrome, she is likely a carrier who will pass on the abnormal X chromosome to her son. Because males have only one X sex chromosome, he will be affected by the syndrome. Her son's genotype will include the abnormal X chromosome. His phenotype will include mental deficiency (ranging from mental retardation to learning disability or short attention span). Scarr's concept of the reaction range states that there is a range of possible phenotypes of each genotype. Therefore, her son will not achieve a high IQ because his genes are constricting that development.   (71–73; 76)

2. Fertility options include:
   a) surgery to correct infertility
   b) hormone based drugs
   c) IVF
   d) GIFT
   e) IUI
   f) ZIFT
   g) ICSI

Adoption is another option.
The pros for fertility options include the possibility of successfully having a baby. Cons of fertility options include an increased risk of multiple births, possible difficulties from infertility surgery, significant monetary burden of any option, and the possibility of the option not resulting in a successful delivery of a baby. The pros for adoption include having a family without subjecting oneself to fertility options, and a lower cost than most IVF techniques. The cons include possible lower levels of adjustment, especially in adoptions of children after the age of 10.   (81–84)

CHAPTER 4: PRENATAL DEVELOPMENT AND BIRTH

A. LEARNING GOALS

Prenatal Development

LG 1: Describe Prenatal Development.

Birth

LG 2: Discuss the Birth Process.

The Postpartum Period

LG 3: Explain the Changes that take place in the Postpartum Period.

B. TRUE OR FALSE KEY CONTENT QUESTIONS

Prenatal Development

1. T F   Prenatal development is divided into three periods: germinal, embryonic, and fetal. (LG 1)

2. T F   The blastocyst is the outer layer of cells that develops during the embryonic period. (LG 1)

3. T F   The placenta is a life-support system connecting arteries and veins to the baby. (LG 1)

4. T F   Organogenesis is the process of organ formation occurring during the first two months of prenatal development. (LG 1)

5. T F   During the fetal period life-support systems develop and organ systems form. (LG 1)

6. T F   The danger of structural defects caused by teratogens is greatest early in embryonic development. (LG 1)

7. T F   Fetal alcohol syndrome can produce abnormalities in the babies of mothers who drank alcohol heavily during pregnancy. (LG 1)

8. T F   Cigarette smoking by pregnant women leads to preterm births and lower birthweights. (LG 1)

9. T F   Because the fetus depends entirely on its mother for nutrition, it is important for the pregnant woman to have good nutritional habits. (LG 1)

10. T F   According to Christine Dunkel-Schetter, there is a strong link between stress during pregnancy and having a high birthweight baby. (LG 1)

Birth

11. T F   At the time of birth, the baby is covered with anoxia, a protective skin grease. (LG 2)

12. T F   A doula, usually a woman, is part of the birthing team who provides continuous physical and emotional support for the mother before, during and after childbirth. (LG 2)

13. T F   An epidural block is an anesthesia that numbs the woman's body from the waist

down. (LG 2)

14. T F   A cesarean section is a delivery of the baby through the abdomen. (LG 2)

15. T F   A preterm infant is one born prior to 40 weeks after conception. (LG 2)

16. T F   Small for date infants are infants whose birth weight is below normal when length of

pregnancy is considered. (LG 2)

17. T F   A low birthweight infant weights less than 6 ½ pounds. (LG 2)

18. T F   The Apgar Scale assesses the health of a newborn by evaluating the infant's size, smell,

and cry. (LG 2)

Postpartum Period

19. T F   The postpartum is the period after childbirth, lasting approximately six months, when the

woman's body adjusts to the process of childbearing. (LG 3)

20. T F   The father also goes through a postpartum adjustment. (LG 3)

C. MATCHING KEY PEOPLE QUESTIONS

___ 1. A French obstetrician who advocated a procedure of a special breathing technique with education on anatomy and physiology. (LG 2)

___ 2. A researcher who has examined the role of touch and massage in development. (LG 2)

___ 3. An obstetrician who developed natural childbirth through breathing and relaxation techniques. (LG 2)

___ 4 Developer of a scale to assess the health of newborns at one and five minutes after birth. (LG 2)

___ 5 Developer of a scale to assess the health of newborns within 24–36 hours after birth. (LG 2)

    A.   Virginia Apgar

    B.   Tiffany Field

    C.   Ferdinand Lamaze

    D.   T. Berry Brazelton

    E.   Ann Streissguth

    F.   Grantley Dick-Read

    G.   Arlene Eisenberg

D. MULTIPLE CHOICE KNOWLEDGE QUESTIONS

1. (LG 1) How does the placenta/umbilical cord life-support system prevent harmful bacteria from invading a fetus?

    a. Bacteria are too large to pass through the placenta's walls.

    b. The placenta generates antibodies that attack and destroy bacteria.

    c. Bacteria become trapped in the maze of blood vessels of the umbilical cord.

    d. No one understands how the placenta keeps bacteria out.

2. (LG 1) The fetal period is best described as a time when

    a. major organ systems emerge from the less differentiated endoderm and mesoderm.

    b. support systems that sustain the fetus become fully formed and functioning.

    c. fine details are added to systems that emerged during the embryonic period.

    d. teratogens are most likely to impair development.

3. (LG 1) Which of the following phrases defines a teratogen?

    a. a life support system that protects the fetus

    b. an agent that stimulates the formation of organs

    c. an abnormality in infants of alcoholics mothers

    d. an environmental factor that produces birth defects

4. (LG 1) Which of the following statements about fetal alcohol syndrome is most accurate?

    a. The infant is often physically deformed and below average in intelligence.

    b. It commonly results in miscarriages.

    c. It causes ectopic pregnancies.

    d. Babies suffering from this syndrome are often born before term and with low birthweights.

5. (LG 1) Which of the following statements about a mother's emotional state and prenatal development is most accurate?

    a. The emotional state of a mother influences prenatal development and birth.

    b. The emotional state of a mother influences birth but not prenatal development.

    c. The emotional state of a mother influences prenatal development but not birth.

    d. The emotional state of a mother has no influence on either prenatal development or birth.

6. (LG 1) Which of the following statements about the relationship between age and pregnancy

    outcomes is most accurate?

    a. Adolescent mothers are most likely to have retarded children.

    b. More women become pregnant through artificial insemination in their thirties and their forties

    than do women in their twenties.

    c. Mothers over age 30 are most likely to have retarded babies.

    d. Adolescent mothers suffer the lowest infant mortality rates of any age group.

7. (LG 2) Mrs. Peters is bearing down hard with each contraction. She is in the _____ stage of

    labor.

    a. first

    b. second

    c. third

    d. final

8. (LG 2) What is the reason for administering analgesics to a woman during labor?

    a. to minimize the risk of cesarean sections

    b. to speed delivery

    c. to facilitate natural childbirth

    d. to lessen the pain for the mother

9. (LG 2) In contrast to the Brazelton scale, the Apgar Scale primarily assesses a newborn's

    a. psychological status.

    b. reflexes.

    c. physiological health.

    d. responsivity to people.

10. (LG 3) Which of the following terms refers to a physical change that occurs to women after childbirth?

   a. decompression

   b. menstruation

   c. involution

   d. natural selection

E. CRITICAL THINKING QUESTIONS

1. Explain how a mother's emotions and experience of stress can influence prenatal development, birth, and the newborn. (LG 1)

2. Why does a breech position complicate the delivery of a baby? (LG 1)

3. How does massage help improve the developmental outcomes of "at-risk" infants? (LG 2)

F. CONCEPTUAL QUESTIONS

1. Design a positive prenatal care program for women who just found out that they are pregnant. In your program, what information would you include to provide education on the topics of teratogens, proper nutrition, emotional states, and prenatal check ups? What additional advice should be given to women over the age of 40? (LG 1)

2. Both women and men need to make adjustments once a baby is born. What suggestions would you make to help both parents adjust to these changes and to foster bonding? (LG 3)

G. APPLICATIONS

1. Interview three couples who have at least one child. What was their childbirth like? What childbirth method or methods were used? How did the overall delivery go? If an APGAR was taken, what was the child's score? What adjustments did both the new mother and new father have to make? Compare their answers to the expectations stated in the book. Also consider interviewing your own parents or caregivers to find out about your delivery into this world.

ANSWER KEY

B. TRUE OR FALSE KEY CONTENT QUESTIONS

1. T (95)
2. F (95)
3. F (95–96)
4. T (96–97)
5. F (96–97)
6. T (99)
7. T (101)
8. T (101)
9. T (105)
10. F (106)
11. F (110–111)
12. T (112)
13. T (112)
14. T (113)
15. F (114)
16. T (114)
17. F (114)
18. F (118)
19. F (119)
20. T (119)

C. MATCHING KEY PEOPLE QUESTIONS
1. C (113)
2. B (117)
3. F (113)
4. A (118)
5. D (118)

D. MULTIPLE CHOICE KNOWLEDGE QUESTIONS

1. a (95–96)
2. c (96–97)
3. d (99)
4. a (101)
5. a (106)
6. c (106)
7. b (110)
8. d (112)
9. c (118)
10. c (119)

E. CRITICAL THINKING QUESTIONS

1. (106)
   - The mother's emotional state can influence the birth process. A stressed-out mother might have irregular contractions and a more difficult labor. This may cause irregularities in the baby's oxygen supply or slower adjustment after birth.
   - Maternal anxiety may result in a hyperactive and irritable infant. The newborn may also have more feeding and sleeping problems. In the Dunkel-Schetter study women under stress are four times more likely to deliver premature babies than low-stress pregnant women.
   - Researchers have found that women who have an optimistic outlook believe they have more control over the outcome of their pregnancy.

2. (114)
   - Normally, the baby's head comes through the vagina first during delivery. However, when the baby's buttocks are the first part to emerge from the vagina, the baby is in a breech position.
   - This position where the head does not come through first can cause respiratory problems. A cesarean delivery, also called cesarean section, is usually performed if the baby is in a breach position.

3. (117)
   - Touch and massage can improve the growth, health and well-being of infants and children. Dr. Tiffany Field's research has demonstrated the benefits of massage in reducing labor pain. Infants who received massage therapy had lower stress, improved sociability, and better gastrointestinal and metabolic efficiency. Massaged infants were also more active and alert. Their hospital stays were six days shorter than nonmassaged babies.

F. CONCEPTUAL QUESTIONS

1. Your positive prenatal care program should be like other prenatal care programs, focusing on comprehensive educational, social, and nutritional services. For each topic, you would inform the expectant mother of the following information:

   a) Teratogens
   - Consult with your physician regarding *any* prescription and nonprescription medication
   - Avoid caffeine, alcohol, and nicotine
   - Do not take *any* illegal drugs
   - Avoid environmental hazards such as pollutants, pesticides, manufacturing chemicals, prolonged exposure to heat in hot tubs, and low level radiation

   b) Nutrition
   - Consume proper doses of proteins, vitamins, and minerals
   - Be sure to add folic acid to your diet

   c) Emotional States
   - Avoid high and/or long levels of stress
   - Try to maintain a positive outlook

   d) Prenatal Checkups
   - Encourage regular prenatal checkups
   - Educate about the different types of prenatal screening and the potential risks associated with each one

For a pregnant woman over the age of 40, you would give the additional education of her having an increased risk of carrying a child with Down Syndrome. (99–109)

2. One overall suggestion is to emphasize that both parents will have some sort of postpartum period of adjustment. For women, they will experience a physical adjustment in their level of energy, changes in hormone production, menstrual cycle, involution, and body contour and strength. Emotionally, they may experience mood swings and are at risk of experiencing the psychological problem of postpartum depression. For men, they will experience adjustments in their usual routine, they may feel left out, and may be worried about being a good parent. Both parents will need to discuss the right time for the resumption of sexual intercourse and ways to promote a good relationship with the baby. Allowing contact with the baby shortly after birth can help promote bonding for both the new mother and father. (119–123)

CHAPTER 5: PHYSICAL, MOTOR, AND PERCEPTUAL DEVELOPMENT IN INFANCY

A. LEARNING GOALS

Physical Growth and Development in Infancy

LG 1: Discuss Physical Growth and Development in Infancy.

Motor Development

LG 2: Describe Infants' Motor Development.

Sensory and Perceptual Development

LG 3: Explain Sensory and Perceptual Development in Infancy.

B. TRUE OR FALSE KEY CONTENT QUESTIONS

Physical Growth and Development in Infancy

1. T F   The sequence in which the greatest physical growth occurs from bottom to top (legs, trunk, head) is called the cephalocaudal pattern. (LG 1)

2. T F   The sequence in which the greatest growth starts at the center of the body and moves toward the extremities is called the proximodistal pattern. (LG 1)

3. T F   From birth to one year of age, infants triple their weight and increase their length by 50 percent. (LG 1)

4. T F   The cerebral cortex plays a critical role in brain functioning, such as perception, thinking, and language. (LG 1)

5. T F   Most adults spend a fourth of their night in REM sleep; most infants spend a third of their night in REM sleep. (LG 1)

6. T F   The American Academy of Pediatrics recommends shared sleeping to promote breast-feeding and detect potentially dangerous breathing pauses in the baby. (LG 1)

7. T F   Sudden infant death syndrome (SIDS) occurs when an infant stops breathing, usually during daytime naps. (LG 1)

8. T F   Nutritionists recommend infants consume 50 calories per day for each pound they weigh. (LG 1)

9. T F   The growing consensus is that bottle-feeding is better for the baby's health during the first six months of life. (LG 1)

Motor Development

10. T F   The sucking reflex enables newborns to get nourishment before they have associated a nipple with food. (LG 2)

11. T F   The rooting reflex occurs when something touches the infant's palms. (LG 2)

12. T   F   The Moro reflex is the infant's response to a loud noise or sudden movement. (LG 2)

13. T   F   The American Academy of Pediatricians recommends structured exercise

     classes for babies to increase coordination and gross motor development. (LG 2)

14. T   F   Infants have to see their own hands when reaching for an object. (LG 2)

15. T   F   Developmental biodynamics emphasizes that perception and action go together when

     new skills are learned. (LG 2)

Sensory and Perceptual Development

16. T   F   Sensation is the interpretation of what is sensed. (LG 3)

17. T   F   Affordances are opportunities for interaction offered by objects that are necessary to

     perform functional activities. (LG 3)

18. T   F   Newborns can see and distinguish colors. (LG 3)

19. T   F   Infants as young as three months have depth perception. (LG 3)

20. T   F   Hearing can occur several weeks before birth in the fetus. (LG 3)

C. MATCHING KEY PEOPLE QUESTIONS

___ 1. A behaviorist who argued that infants should be fed on a schedule rather than on demand. (LG 1)

___ 2. An experimenter who used the looking chamber to determine the visual preferences of infants. (LG 2)

___ 3. A researcher who demonstrated that young infants form visual expectations. (LG 3)

___ 4. A psychologist who described a newborn's perceptual world as "blooming, buzzing confusion". (LG 3)

___ 5. A psychologist who argued that individuals perceive in order to move and move in order to perceive. (LG 3)

___ 6. Researchers who used the visual cliff to study infant perception. (LG 3)

___ 7. A pediatrician who observed infants to determine the incidence of their sucking when they were nursing and how their sucking changed over time. (LG 2)

___ 8. A researcher who found that infants do not have to see their hands when reaching for an object. (LG 2)

___ 9. A researcher who studied the benefits of nutritional supplements in children living in Guatemala. (LG 2)

___ 10. Researchers who promote the ecological view of perception. (LG 3)

A   Ernesto Pollitt

B.   Esther Thelen

C.   T. Berry Brazelton

D.   John Breur

E.   Robert Fantz

F.   Eleanor Gibson and Richard Walk

G.   Elizabeth Spelke

H.   Rachel Clifton

I.   John Watson

J.   Eleanor Gibson and James J. Gibson

K.   William James

D. MULTIPLE CHOICE KNOWLEDGE QUESTIONS

1. (LG 1) Which principles explain why an embryo's hands develop before its fingers, and why the head develops before the body?

    a. cephalocaudal, cephalocaudal

    b. cephalocaudal, proximodistal

    c. proximodistal, cephalocaudal

    d. proximodistal, proximodistal

2. (LG 1) Which of the following statements most accurately describes height and weight changes during infancy?

    a. Both increase more rapidly during the second year than during the first year.

    b. Girls increase in height and weight faster than do boys during infancy.

    c. The sexes grow at the same rate during infancy.

    d. Both height and weight increase more rapidly during the first year than during the second year.

3. (LG 1) Developmentalists have hypothesized that the large amount of REM sleep in infants

    a. is a dream state related to infant fears.

    b. is a symbolic return to the womb.

    c. is caused by the need to eat or eliminate.

    d. is a form of self-stimulation.

4. (LG 1) Juan was a low-birthweight infant, whereas Billy was a premature infant. Which of the following statements applies to them?

    a. Neither is vulnerable to SIDS.

    b. Juan is less vulnerable to SIDS than Billy.

    c. Juan is more vulnerable to SIDS than Billy.

    d. Both are vulnerable to SIDS.

5. (LG 1) Jill's parents followed John Watson's advice about feeding, and Jack's parents followed today's trend. Which schedule did they use, respectively?

    a. scheduled feeding; demand feeding

    b. demand feeding; scheduled feeding

    c. bottle-feeding; breast-feeding

    d. breast-feeding; bottle-feeding

6. (LG 1) Which dietary element will health-conscious parents omit from their baby's diets if they do not study infants' dietary needs?

    a. protein

    b. carbohydrates

    c. fat

    d. sugar

7. (LG 2) Which statement best characterizes infant reflexes?

    a. Infants once needed reflexes but no longer do.

    b. Reflexes are genetically coded survival mechanisms for all infants.

    c. Modern infants rely more on learning than on reflexes.

    d. All reflexes disappear by the end of infancy.

8. (LG 3) When infants were placed on one side of the visual cliff, they refused to go to their mothers who were coaxing them from the other side. This result was cited as evidence for which of the following?

    a. depth perception

    b. failure of visual acuity

    c. inability to hear at a distance

    d. inability to crawl

9. (LG 3) What evidence indicates that a fetus can hear?

    a. A fetus moves when a loud noise occurs.

    b. Newborns prefer their mother's voice to a stranger's voice.

    c. Hearing is more sensitive and better developed among newborns who have been experimentally stimulated before birth.

    d. Newborns prefer to hear stories that were read to them just before they were born.

10. (LG 3) When an infant turns its head at the sound of footsteps in the hall and then smiles when it sees Mom come into the room, the infant is using

    a. depth perception.

    b. intermodal perception.

    c. auditory perception.

    d. visual perception.

E. CRITICAL THINKING QUESTIONS

1. Explain why infants spend so much time in REM sleep. (LG 1)

2. Discuss the pros and cons of breast-feeding versus bottle-feeding. (LG 1)

3. What is appropriate exercise for infants? (LG 2)

F. CONCEPTUAL QUESTIONS

1. Explain how brain development is promoted in infants. (LG 1)

2. Brianna is a one-month-old infant whose bedroom has pale pink walls. On one wall, there are two large pictures of balloons – one yellow, and one red. On another wall is a picture of a cartoon zebra. How will Brianna respond to this room? How will her response change when she is six months old? (LG 3)

G. APPLICATIONS

Visit an infant daycare center and rate how well it (a) organizes activities to promote infant physical development and (b) decorates its walls to relate to infant capabilities. How might you design the ideal infant daycare center?

ANSWER KEY

B. TRUE OR FALSE KEY CONTENT QUESTIONS

1. F (131)
2. T (132)
3. T (132)
4. T (134–135)
5. F (137)
6. F (137)
7. F (138)
8. T (139)
9. F (140)
10. T (144)
11. F (144)
12. T (144)
13. F (148)
14. F (149–150)
15. T (151)
16. F (152)
17. T (152–153)
18. T (153)
19. F (156–157)
20. T (157)

C. MATCHING KEY PEOPLE QUESTIONS

1. I (139)
2. E (154)
3. G (156–157)
4. K (153)
5. B (160)
6. F (155–156)
7. C (145)
8. H (149–150)
9. A (143)
10. J (152–153)

D. MULTIPLE CHOICE KNOWLEDGE QUESTIONS

1. c (131–132)
2. d (132)
3. d (137)
4. d (138–139)
5. a (139)
6. c (139)
7. b (144)
8. a (155–156)
9. d (157)
10. b (159)

E. CRITICAL THINKING QUESTIONS

1. (137)
    - The amount of Rapid Eye Movement (REM) sleep changes over the life span. Approximately 50 percent of an infant's sleep is REM sleep. Most adults spend only 20 percent of the night in REM sleep and elderly adults drop to less than 15 percent. Since infants sleep approximately 16 hours per day, the large amount of REM sleep may provide stimulation necessary for brain development.

2. (139–140)
    - Breast-feeding provides human milk that is clean and digestible and helps immunize the newborn from disease. Breast-fed babies gain weight more rapidly. However, only half of mothers nurse newborns. Mothers who work outside the home find it difficult to breast-feed infants. Also, there is no evidence that bottle-fed infants suffer physiological or psychological harm. Many parents, especially working mothers, breast feed during the first few months (often using a pump to extract breast milk that can be stored for a later feeding) of the newborn's life and bottle-feed thereafter.

3. (148–149)
    - Although toddlers are quite active, pediatricians do not recommend structured exercise. It is easy to go beyond the infant's physical limitations without knowing it and cause dislocations.
    - Exercise for infants is not aerobic. They cannot adequately stretch their bodies at this age.
    - It is better to engage infants in passive exercise that encourage such appropriate physical development as pushing, pulling, crawling, etc.

F. CONCEPTUAL QUESTIONS

1. Infant brain development is promoted by early experience, sleep, and nutrition (156–157):
    a) early experience
    - infant environment should be stimulating to promote neural connections
    - infants who grow up in a deprived environment have problems with their cognitive development

    b) sleep
    - REM sleep helps promote cognitive development
    - infants need a lot of REM sleep

    c) nutrition
    - breast-feeding helps neurological and cognitive development
    - malnutrition is detrimental to brain development
    - early nutritional supplements of protein and increased calories can promote cognitive development

2. Brianna's vision is between 20/400 – 20/800. She can distinguish between red and green but not other colors. As a result, she will likely see her pale pink walls as gray. She will have trouble focusing on the pictures in her room, but she'll prefer looking at the zebra to the balloons. She will notice the red balloon, but not the yellow balloon. At six months, her vision has improved and she is now able to notice her pink walls and the yellow balloon. She will still prefer the zebra or any other pattern to the balloons because she is more interested in patterns than a picture with no pattern. (153–157)

CHAPTER 6: PHYSICAL DEVELOPMENT IN CHILDHOOD AND ADOLESCENCE

A. LEARNING GOALS

Physical Growth in Childhood

LG 1: Discuss Physical Growth in Childhood.

Health and Illness

LG 2: Describe Children's and Adolescents' Health and Illness.

Puberty and Adolescence

LG 3: Explain the Changes of Puberty and Adolescence.

B. TRUE OR FALSE KEY CONTENT QUESTIONS

Physical Growth in Childhood

1. T F   The average child grows over 2 1/2 inches in height and gains 5–7 pounds a year

during early childhood. (LG 1)

2. T F   Children double their strength capacity during middle and late childhood. (LG 1)

3. T F   Running, swimming, cycling, and hiking are recommended exercises for children. (LG 1)

4. T F   Boys are usually better at gross motor skills and girls are better at fine motor skills during

middle and late childhood. (LG 1)

5. T F   Myelination is the insulation of fat over the nerve cells that dampens the speed of

information traveling through the nervous system. (LG 1)

6. T F   An average preschool child requires 2,400 calories per day. (LG 1)

Health and Illness

7. T F   Obesity results in both physical and psychological problems. (LG 2)

8. T F   Most anorexics are from lower-income families. (LG 2)

9. T F   Cancer is the second leading cause of death in children 5–14 years old. (LG 2)

10. T F   Leukemia is the most common form of childhood cancer. (LG 2)

11. T F   Suicide is the second leading cause of death in adolescence. (LG 2)

Puberty and Adolescence

12. T   F   Menarche has been increasing an average of 4 months per decade. (LG 3)

13. T   F   On the average, puberty begins and peaks two years earlier for girls than boys. (LG 3)

14. T   F   Girls are less happy with their bodies and have more negative body images than

boys. (LG 3)

15. T   F   Early-maturing boys are more likely to smoke, drink, be depressed, have older

friends, and request earlier independence. (LG 3)

16. T   F   Most young adolescents have had sexual intercourse by age 15. (LG 3)

17. T   F   Recent trends indicate adolescents are increasing their use of contraceptives. (LG 3)

18. T   F   Alcohol is the most widely used drug by adolescents. (LG 3)

19. T   F   Parents who set limits on adolescents' activities are more likely to have adolescents who

use drugs. (LG 3)

20. T   F   Successful intervention/prevention programs include early identification, individual

attention, and community-wide intervention. (LG 3)

C. MATCHING KEY PEOPLE QUESTIONS

___ 1. Successful left-handed individuals. (LG 1)

___ 2. A national polling organization that surveys adolescent sexual behavior. (LG 3)

___ 3. A family consumer science educator who teaches life skills to adolescents. (LG 3)

___ 4. Researchers who reported that public attitudes about adolescents emerge from a combination

of personal experience and media portrayals. (LG 3)

___ 5. Researchers who monitored drug use by American secondary students. (LG 3)

___ 6. An adolescent health expert who developed a life skills education curriculum. (LG 2)

A. Lloyd Johnston, Patrick O'Malley, and Gerald Bachman

B. Alan Guttmacher Institute

C. David Hamburg

D. Leonardo Da Vinci, Benjamin Franklin, and Pablo Picasso

E. Lynn Blankenship

F. Heart Smart

G. Shirley Feldman & Glen Elliott

H. P. Lindsay Chase-Lansdale

I. Daniel Yankelovich

J. Joy Dryfoos

D. MULTIPLE CHOICE KNOWLEDGE QUESTIONS

1. (LG 1) Deprivation dwarfism is a type of growth retardation caused by

    a. prenatal problems.

    b. nutritional deprivation.

    c. emotional deprivation.

    d. problems with the hypothalamus.

2. (LG 1) Which pattern best portrays changes in gross and fine motor skills in middle and late childhood?

    a. Girls out-perform boys in gross motor skills.

    b. Boys out-perform girls in gross motor skills.

    c. There are no sex differences in the development of gross and fine motor skills.

    d. Boys out-perform girls in fine motor skills.

3. (LG 1) Which of the following would be considered a fine motor skill?

    a. bouncing a ball

    b. walking a straight line

    c. stacking blocks

    d. throwing a ball overhand

4. (LG 1) Which behavior of newborns predicts hand preference later in life?

    a. direction of eye gaze

    b. direction of head turning

    c. consistent use of one hand to grab things

    d. tendency to roll to the right or left

5. (LG 1) Myelination improves the efficiency of the central nervous system the way that

    a. talking to an infant speeds his ability to produce a first word.

    b. reducing the distance between two children playing catch reduces the time it takes for a baseball to travel from one child to the other.

    c. the ingestion of certain chemicals (e.g., steroids) can improve overall muscle development.

    d. the insulation around an electrical extension cord improves the efficiency.

6. (LG 2) What is the most effective way for parents to promote good fitness habits in their children?

  a. Encourage children to play competitive sports.

  b. Involve the entire family in a vigorous exercise program.

  c. Limit the time spent watching television.

  d. Create a substantial challenge for children, such as training for a marathon.

7. (LG 2) Which of the following is one health problem children might experience if exposed to parental smoke?

  a. asthma

  b. low vitamin B

  c. influenza

  d. Attention Deficit Hyperactivity Disorder

8. (LG 3) The most noticeable changes in body growth for females include all of the following *except*

  a. height spurt.

  b. tendencies towards obesity.

  c. breast growth.

  d. menarche.

9. (LG 3) According to Kinsey, the percentage of adolescent males who are homosexual is

  a. 10 percent

  b. 8 percent

  c. 4 percent

  d. 2 percent

10. (LG 3) Infants born to adolescent mothers are more likely to have

    a. neurological problems.

    b. low birthweight.

    c. childhood illness.

    d. All of the above are correct.

11. (LG 3) In order to be classified as a "very high-risk youth," 15-year-old Wayne would have to

    a. commit a serious crime.

    b. be a heavy drug user.

    c. be sexually active, but not using contraceptives.

    d. All of the above are correct.

12. (LG 3) Which of the following is *not* a component of successful programs for reducing adolescent problems?

    a. intensive individualized attention

    b. early identification and intervention

    c. community-wide multiagency collaborative approaches

    d. involvement of the whole family

E. CRITICAL THINKING QUESTIONS

1. What are the positive and negative consequences for children's participation in sports? (LG 2)

2. Describe the gender differences in adolescents' perceptions of their bodies. (LG 3)

F. CONCEPTUAL QUESTIONS

1. A father of two children, one a preschooler and one an adolescent, wants to know how to improve the health of his children. What can he do for each child, factoring in the children's level of cognitive ability? (LG 2)

2. What advice would you give a mother who is worried about her adolescent daughter possibly abusing drugs? (LG 3)

G. APPLICATIONS

Think back to when you were an adolescent. How would you describe that time in your life? How did your development compare to what is mentioned in the textbook in regards to (a) puberty, (b) hormonal changes, (c) height, weight, and sexual maturation, and (d) body image?

ANSWER KEY

B. TRUE OR FALSE KEY CONTENT QUESTIONS

1. T (169)
2. T (170)
3. T (171)
4. T (171–172)
5. F (173)
6. F (176–177)
7. T (177)
8. F (179)
9. T (181–182)
10. T (181–182)
11. F (182)
12. F (183)
13. T (185–186)
14. T (186–187)
15. F (187)
16. F (188–189)
17. T (189–190)
18. T (192)
19. F (195)
20. T (195–196)

C. MATCHING KEY PEOPLE QUESTIONS

1. D (172)
2. B (188–189)
3. E (191)
4. G (196–197)
5. A (192)
6. C (176)

D. MULTIPLE CHOICE KNOWLEDGE QUESTIONS

1. c (169–170)
2. b (171)
3. c (171)
4. b (172)
5. d (173)
6. b (179–180)
7. a (180–181)
8. b (183–186)
9. c (188)
10. d (191)
11. d (195–196)
12. d (195–196)

E. CRITICAL THINKING QUESTIONS

1. (180)
    - Children's participation in sports can provide exercise, physical skill development, and a setting to develop friendships. However, sports can also have a negative impact when adults stress unrealistic expectation to win. When ambitious parents or organizations push children to engage in long and arduous training to achieve success, a distorted (and exploitive) view

62

of sports gets communicated to the child. Ideally, sports participation is an opportunity for a child to increase physical strength, develop motor coordination, and improve flexibility.

2.   (186–187)
- One universal aspect of adolescence is a preoccupation with their bodies and their body image. During puberty adolescents are acutely sensitive to the changes in their body image. Generally, adolescent girls are less happy with their body image than are boys. During late puberty body fat increases. This is certainly a tender spot for adolescent girls. Later- maturing girls are taller and thinner and, by tenth grade, are more satisfied with their bodies.

- During late puberty, body muscle mass increases. This would be viewed as desirable by adolescent boys. Longitudinal studies indicate that late-maturing boys develop a stronger sense of identity than early-maturing boys. Since they had a long lead time regarding their physical development, late-maturing boys had more time to focus on personal achievement and career aspirations.

F. CONCEPTUAL QUESTIONS

1. For his preschool child, any type of program should be cognitively simple. There are three simple but important goals for healthcare programs for preschool children:
    a) help children identify feelings of wellness and illness and be able to express them to adults
    b) help children identify appropriate sources of assistance for health-related problems
    c) help children independently initiate the use of sources of assistance for health problems
His adolescent child has greater cognitive skills but also has a sense of uniqueness and invulnerability that places him or her at risk for many health problems. The father will need to consider this as he provides his child with a life science education program that reviews puberty, reproductive systems, sexual behavior, sexually transmitted diseases, nutrition, diet and exercise. He might also encourage a life skills program.

The father can help both children by controlling the speed of his car, decreasing his drinking, refraining from smoking around the children, monitoring their safety, ensuring they have proper nutrition, and maintaining their dental hygiene. One other suggestion is to make sure his children get the proper amount of exercise to decrease the risk of obesity. (174–175)

2. You might advise this mother that her concerns are valid. She might want to be aware of her daughter being drawn to drugs (including club drugs), alcohol, and cigarette smoking. She should watch how her daughter copes with stress, making sure the daughter is not using substances as a means to cope. She should keep a positive relationship with her daughter and continue to set limits on curfews and television/Internet content. (191–195)

SECTION 3: COGNITION AND LANGUAGE

CHAPTER 7: COGNITIVE DEVELOPMENTAL APPROACHES

A. LEARNING GOALS

Piaget's Cognitive Developmental Theory

LG 1: Discuss Piaget's Place in Developmental Psychology and the Key Dimensions of His Theory.

Piaget's Stages

LG 2: Describe Piaget's Four Stages of Cognitive Development.

Applying and Evaluating Piaget's Theory

LG 3: Apply Piaget's Theory to Education and Evaluate his Theory.

Vygotsky's Theory of Cognitive Development

LG 4: Summarize Vygotsky's Theory and Compare It with Piaget's Theory.

TRUE OR FALSE KEY CONTENT QUESTIONS

Piaget's Cognitive Developmental Theory

1. T F Assimilation occurs when children adjust to new information. (LG 1)

2. T F Piaget's concept of grouping behavior into higher-order levels of thought is called organization. (LG 1)

Piaget's Stages

3. T F It is the similar way of understanding the world that makes one stage more advanced than another in Piaget's stages of cognitive development. (LG 2)

4. T F Simple reflexes are one characteristic of the sensorimotor stage. (LG 2)

5. T F Object permanence is one of the infant's most important accomplishments. (LG 2)

6. T F If infants are surprised at the disappearance of an object, it is assumed they believe it continues to exist. (LG 2)

7. T F Recent research on infant cognitive development suggests that infants' perceptual abilities happen later than Piaget first believed. (LG 2)

8. T F Operations are externalized actions that allow a child to do physically what before he or she did mentally. (LG 2)

9. T F An example of animism is a child saying, "The sidewalk made me fall down." (LG 2)

10. T F In the preoperational thought stage, the child lacks a sense of conservation and asks a ton of questions. (LG 2)

11. T F In the concrete operational thought stage, a child can engage in reversible mental action on real concrete objects, like different shapes of clay. (LG 2)

12. T F The concrete operational child still has difficulty with seriation. (LG 2)

13. T F In the formal operational thought stage, hypothetical-deductive reasoning is the means for problem-solving. (LG 2)

14. T F Adolescents think about ideal characteristics of themselves, others, and the world. (LG 2)

Applying and Evaluating Piaget's Theory

15. T F One way Piaget's theory has been applied to education is to consider the child's knowledge and level of thinking. (LG 3)

16. T F One criticism of Piaget's theory concerns developmental synchrony, that is, that various aspects of a stage emerge continuously. (LG 3)

Vygotsky's Theory of Cognitive Development

17. T F The lower limit zone of proximal development (ZPD) represents tasks a child can accomplish with the assistance of a more skilled person. (LG 4)

18. T F Scaffolding means changing the level of support by using a more skilled person for help. (LG 4)

19. T F Vygotsky believed that young children use language for self-regulation such as inner speech or private speech. (LG 4)

20. T F Vygotsky believed that self-talk reflects immaturity. (LG 4)

B. MATCHING KEY PEOPLE QUESTIONS

___ 1. A psychologist who developed the conceptual framework of cognitive development. (LG 1)

___ 2. Researcher who believes that personal fable and imaginary audience help define an adolescent's sense of uniqueness. (LG 2)

___ 3. A psychologist who believes that attention is an important explanation for conservation, and that conservation appears earlier than Piaget thought. (LG 2)

___ 4. A developmental psychologist who argues that guided participation, especially in cultural activities, is an important aspect of children's development. (LG 4)

___ 5. A psychologist who found that infants look at impossible events longer than possible events. (LG 2)

A. Jean Piaget

B. Rochel Gelman

C. Renee Baillargeon

D. Marshall Haith

E. David Elkind

F. Daniel Keating

G. Gisela Labouvie-Vief

H. John Flavell

I. Lev Vygotsky

J. Barbara Rogoff

C. MULTIPLE CHOICE KNOWLEDGE QUESTIONS

1. (LG 1) Organization and _____ enable a child to effectively interact with the environment.

    a. accommodation

    b. adaptation

    c. assimilation

    d. schema

2. (LG 1) If Linda tries to incorporate new features of the environment into her thinking by modifying existing schemes, she is using

    a. organization.

    b. adaptation.

    c. assimilation.

    d. accommodation.

3. (LG 1) Which of the following Piagetian concepts explains how children shift from one stage of thought to the next?

    a. assimilation

    b. organization

    c. adaptation

    d. equilibrium

4. (LG 2) Nancy's handkerchief was blown away by the wind. She was heard to say, "The wind is mean and wants to steal my hanky." This is evidence of _____ thought.

    a. egocentric

    b. symbolic

    c. intuitive

    d. animistic

5. (LG 2) Concrete operations allow the child to

    a. mentally construct hypotheses and theories.

    b. imagine the necessary steps in solving a problem.

    c. coordinate several characteristics rather than focus on a single property of an object.

    d. imagine and analyze the thoughts of others compared to the thoughts of himself.

6. (LG 2) The formal-operational thinker is

    a. more tied to reality than the preoperational or concrete-operational child who uses a sort of pseudo-logic.

    b. exceptionally insightful about the practical aspects of life.

    c. demanding of a literally true answer to most problems.

    d. capable of abstraction.

7. (LG 2) Kim, an adolescent, is walking down the hallway of her school and is certain that everyone is watching her. This is an example of

    a. a personal fable.

    b. an adolescent paranoia.

    c. an imaginary audience.

    d. All of the above are correct.

8. (LG 3) Piaget's theory has been criticized on the basis that

   a. the concepts are not very interesting.

   b. children do not seem to behave the way he described.

   c. the idea of development following a series of stages has not been well supported by the evidence.

   d. assimilation and accommodation do not work the way he described.

9. (LG 4) Margo is teaching Tom to play a new composition for the piano. Initially Margo must provide each explanation, many hints, and several demonstrations. As Tom practices, Margo's instruction is reduced. Gradually Tom learns to perform the composition well all by himself. This is an example of Lev Vygotsky's concept of

   a. assimilation.

   b. wisdom.

   c. apprenticeship training.

   d. scaffolding

10. (LG 4) Which of the following is *not* a way that Vygotsky's theory can be incorporated in the classroom?

    a. Teach to the child's zone of proximal development

    b. Use scaffolding

    c. Promote the student's intellectual health

    d. Encourage children's use of private speech

E. CRITICAL THINKING QUESTIONS

1. Imagine a conversation between a four year old and a 15 year old about how a rainbow appears and then disappears. Explain how their perceptions would differ using Piaget's stage theory. (LG 2)

2. Describe how neo-Piagetians would revise Piaget's original theory. (LG 3)

3. Piaget is considered a cognitive constructivist. Vygotsky is considered a social constructivist. Compare and contrast their theories as they apply to teaching and learning. (LG 3 and 4)

F. CONCEPTUAL QUESTIONS

1. Kobe is a two-year-old child. Trace his cognitive development over the past 24 months according to Piaget's theory. What accomplishments did he achieve? Include information from recent researchers such as Spelke and Baillargeon. (LG 2)

2. Using Vygotsky's theory, how would you help a child who is having difficulties with academic subjects in school? (LG 4)

G. APPLICATIONS

Try to find two children between the ages of four and eight to test out the accuracy of Piaget's theory. Make sure you have the permission of the parents and include them in your "mini-experiments". On each child, do the (1) conservation of liquid and (2) conservation of mass (play dough) task. What were your results? Were there age differences? Did the findings match what was expected for that age? If you cannot find children to do these tests on, get permission to observe children at a nearby school. Observe the children's behaviors and conversations and try to identify examples that fit Piaget's description of cognitive development. Also note abilities or task achievements that appear to reflect a higher level of functioning than Piaget described in his theory.

ANSWER KEY

B. TRUE OR FALSE KEY CONTENT QUESTIONS

1. F (207)
2. T (207–208)
3. F (209)
4. T (209)
5. T (210–211)
6. T (211)
7. F (214)
8. F (214–215)
9. T (215)
10. T (214–219)
11. T (220)
12. F (220–221)
13. T (222)
14. T (224–225)
15. T (227)
16. F (229)
17. F (229–230)
18. T (230)
19. T (230)
20. F (232)

C. MATCHING KEY PEOPLE QUESTIONS

1. A (207)
2. E (224–225)
3. B (219)
4. J (231)
5. C (211)

D. MULTIPLE CHOICE KNOWLEDGE QUESTIONS

1. b (207)
2. d (207)
3. d (207–208)
4. d (215–216)
5. c (220)
6. d (220–221)
7. c (224)
8. b (228)
9. d (229–230)
10. c (232–233)

D. CRITICAL THINKING QUESTIONS

1. (214–215; 220–222)
   - The perception of the four year old is guided by preoperational thought. It is characterized by egotism and animism. The child's perception is intuitive, and he is unaware of how he knows. Accordingly, the rainbow comes because it is beautiful. It leaves when it is no longer beautiful.
   - The perception of the fifteen year old is guided by formal thought. It is characterized by abstract, idealistic, and logical thought. Adolescents are capable of hypothetical-deductive reasoning, but develop a kind of egocentrism that involves an imaginary audience and personal fable about being unique and invulnerable. Accordingly, they will describe a rainbow coming from the combination of rain and sunlight. They might also speak of the myth of a pot of gold at the end of the rainbow.

2. (222)
   - More emphasis given to information processing strategies such as attention and memory.
   - More emphasis given to the speed at which children process information.
   - More emphasis given to the type and complexity of tasks.
   - More emphasis given to problem-solving, especially dividing tasks into smaller steps.

3. (227–232)
   - Piaget believed that children learn best when they actively seek solutions for themselves. Therefore, the classroom should be turned into an environment of exploration and discovery. Children's intellectual growth would be promoted through peer interaction with naturalistic activities. Example: A math lesson is constructed around counting the number of days until Christmas.
   - Vygotsky believed that education plays a central role in helping children develop necessary cultural tools. Like Piaget, he believed that the teacher was more of a facilitator than a director. However, his views on the sociocultural development of children are more relevant and accessible, especially using the ZPD to improve children's literacy. Example: A reading lesson is reinforced using cross-aged tutors.

F. CONCEPTUAL QUESTIONS

1. Kobe began his cognitive development through the exercising of his simple reflexes. This was followed by the formation of habits centered on his body, such as sucking his thumb. He then formed habits using external objects, such as shaking a rattle. Prior to his first birthday, Kobe was able to coordinate his learned schemes and intentionally accomplish goals. He then became very curious about his environment and novel objects. Finally, he was able to begin symbolizing events in his head. Recent researchers would view Kobe's infancy period as involving his seeing objects as bounded, unitary, solid, and separate from their background. (209–211)

2. The following Vygotsky concepts could be used to help that child (230–233):
   a) Assess the child's zone of proximal development to see what activities he can accomplish on his own (lower limit) and which activities he can achieve with the assistance of a more skilled person (upper limit).
   b) You would use scaffolding when teaching new concepts to the child. As the child understood more about the concept, your level of directed learning would decrease.
   c) You could also assign a cognitive apprentice for the child.
   d) Finally, you would encourage the child's use of private speech when solving problems.

CHAPTER 8: INFORMATION PROCESSING

A. LEARNING GOALS

The Information Processing Approach

LG 1: Discuss the Basic Ideas in the Information Processing Approach and Compare It with the Cognitive Developmental Approach.

Memory

LG 2: Describe the Way that Memory Works in Children.

Thinking

LG 3: Explain How Children Think.

Metacognition

LG 4: Summarize Developmental Changes and Processes Involved in Children's Metacognition.

TRUE OR FALSE KEY CONTENT QUESTIONS

The Information Processing Approach

1. T F   The information-processing approach focuses on memory and thinking. (LG 1)

2. T F   Encoding refers to how computers store and retrieve information. (LG 1)

3. T F   Automaticity refers to the ability to process information with little or no effort. (LG 1)

4. T F   Metacognition refers to self-awareness about cognition, that is, "knowing about

                knowing." (LG 1)

Memory

5. T F   In terms of information-processing, attention refers to the formal posture of soldiers

                during individual or group presentation. (LG 2)

6. T F   Dishabituation means a renewed interest in a stimulus. (LG 2)

7. T F   Young children tend to focus more on what is important rather than a task or

                situation. (LG 2)

8. T F   Younger children are better at deploying attention than older children because they are

                more likely to construct a plan of action. (LG 2)

9. T F   Rehearsal is the conscious repetition of information over time that keeps the information

                in memory longer. (LG 2)

10. T F   The theory "levels of processing" suggests that deeper processing produces better

                memory. (LG 2)

11. T F   Self-reference is a way to elaborate information. (LG 2)

12. T F   Short-term memory lasts about 30 seconds. (LG 2)

13. T F   The faster six year olds repeated auditorially presented words, the shorter were their

                memory spans. (LG 2)

14. T F   Procedural memory is the conscious recollection of information such as facts or

                events. (LG 2)

15. T F   In areas where children are experts, their memory can exceed that of adults who are

            novices in that content area. (LG 2)

16. T F   A script is a schema for an event. (LG 2)

17. T F   Interference theory asserts that we forget not because we lose memories, but because

            other information gets in the way of what we are trying to remember. (LG 2)

18. T F   The emotional blows of personal trauma can produce distortions of memory or repression

            to the unconscious mind. (LG 2)

Thinking

19. T F   Concepts are elements of the affect that demonstrate the complexity of emotions of

            common properties. (LG 3)

20. T F   Working backwards in time helps establish subgoals for problem solving. (LG 3)

21. T F   Heuristics are strategies that guarantee an answer to a problem. (LG 3)

22. T F   Critical thinking involves thinking productively and evaluating the evidence, but does not

            involve reflection. (LG 3)

Metacognition

23. T F   Metacognitive knowledge involves monitoring and reflecting on one's current

            thoughts. (LG 4)

24. T F   High achieving students who set more specific learning goals are modeling self-

            regulatory strategies. (LG 4)

B. MATCHING KEY PEOPLE QUESTIONS

___ 1. Investigator who illustrated the importance of rehearsal and developmental change. (LG 2)

___ 2. Cognitive psychologist who identified two types of declarative memory: episodic and semantic. (LG 2)

___ 3. A researcher who believes that memories are stored as a verbal code or an image code. (LG 2)

___ 4. Proposed that explicit memory does not occur until the second half of the first year. (LG 2)

___ 5. A researcher who argued infants as young as two to six months of age can remember some experiences through one-and-a-half to two years. (LG 2)

___ 6. A developmentalist who observed deferred imitation by infants. (LG 3)

___ 7. A memory researcher who is skeptical about repressed memory of child abuse. (LG 2)

___ 8. Leading theorist who described three main characteristics of the information-processing approach. (LG 1)

___ 9. Demonstrated children between the ages of one and five are capable of some type of analogical reasoning. (LG 3)

___ 10. Want teachers to promote critical thinking in classrooms. (LG 4)

A.   Robert Siegler

B.   Carilyn Rovee-Collier

C.   John Flavell

D.   Allan Paivio

E.   Endel Tulving

F.   Elizabeth Loftus

G.   Ann Brown

H.   John Bransford

I.   Max Wertheimer

J.   Deanna Kuhn

K.   David Perkins and Sarah Tishman

L.   Jean Mandler

M.   Andrew Meltzoff

C. MULTIPLE CHOICE KNOWLEDGE QUESTIONS

1. (LG 1) The _____ approach deals with how individuals analyze their many sources of information and the numerous steps used to make sense of this information.

   a. critical thinking

   b. information-processing

   c. cognitive monitoring

   d. decisional

2. (LG 1) Ten-year-old MaiLee lives in Hong Kong and quickly reads the local newspaper every day. Her seven-year-old brother takes much longer as he tries to say unfamiliar words out loud. In other words, compared to her brother, MaiLee exhibits greater

   a. automaticity.

   b. processing capacity.

   c. word processing.

   d. encoding.

3. (LG 2) A child's ability to focus on a parent's instructions even though baby brother is crying and the television is blaring is called

   a. encoding.

   b. attention.

   c. automaticity.

   d. memory.

4. (LG 2) Josie is a newborn whose older brother keeps coming up to her crib and saying "hi" while she is trying to take a nap. At first, Josie kept waking up to her brother but now she remains asleep. This behavior is called

    a. habituation

    b. dishabituation

    c. elaboration

    d. procedural memory

5. (LG 2) When asked to judge whether two complex pictures are the same, preschool children will

    a. correctly indicate the pictures are the same.

    b. systematically compare the details across the pictures.

    c. use a haphazard comparison strategy.

    d. be able to shift their attention from one picture to another.

6. (LG 2) Which of the following is not one of the three levels of processing according to Craik and Lockhart?

    a. initial

    b. shallow

    c. intermediate

    d. deepest

7. (LG 2) The type of memory that lasts for a fraction of a second to several seconds is

    a. sensory memory

    b. working memory

    c. short-term memory

    d. long-term memory

8. (LG 2) The directions for turning on the Nintendo game, Grandma's full name, and Marian's favorite flavor of ice-cream are

    a. stored in long-term memory.

    b. aspects of short-term memory.

    c. elements of sensory memory, as long as rehearsal occurs.

    d. examples of cognitive monitoring.

9. (LG 2) Knowing what you had for dinner last night is an example of _____ memory.

    a. semantic

    b. declarative

    c. procedural

    d. episodic

10. (LG 2) Which of the following is *not* a characteristic of an expert?

    a. Notices meaningful patterns of information that novices do not notice

    b. Has a superior recall in their area of expertise

    c. Has no need for practice in area of expertise

    d. Retrieves information with little effort

11. (LG 2) Both you and your professor have to deliver talks at two different high schools on "How Babies Learn to Talk." Your professor, an expert on language acquisition, is likely to spend most of her preparation time

    a. gathering information.

    b. rehearsing the completed speech.

    c. planning in her mind what she wants to communicate and how.

    d. sitting by the computer trying to organize facts.

12. (LG 2) When asked what happens at a birthday party, Chrissy is clear that, "First you put on hats, then you play, then you sing Happy Birthday, and then you eat cake. Last you open." Chrissy is recounting a(n)

    a. schema.

    b. script.

    c. semantic network.

    d. heuristic.

13. (LG 3) Programs about child-sexual abuse prevention often spend a great deal of time distinguishing between "good-touch" and "bad-touch." These programs are attempting to teach the child

    a. expertise.

    b. novice.

    c. concepts.

    d. metacognition.

14. (LG 3) The infant who is providing an example of deferred imitation is one who

    a. sticks out his tongue whenever he sees his mother stick out her tongue.

    b. appears to innately organize items into groups of two's.

    c. sees his mom wave goodbye to his dad and two hours later waves his hand just like his mom did.

    d. continues to stare at his crib mobile even though it has just stopped spinning.

15. (LG 3) All of the following are important elements of critical thinking *except*

    a. evaluating the similarities and differences between things.

    b. evaluating and understanding statements rather than just accepting them.

    c. applying "commonsense" and everyday knowledge to new problems.

    d. judging valid and invalid inferences from data.

16. (LG 4) Twelve-year-old Laura decides to wait to tell her parents about her poor math grade after the dinner with her mother's boss. She knows that telling her them before dinner will disturb their ability to enjoy the dinner party. Here Laura is displaying her

    a. schemas about relationships with supervisors.

    b. semantic network about how parents behave.

    c. metacognitions about people.

    d. information processing strategies.

17. (LG 4) One helpful way to get young children to use strategies is to

    a. use mental imagery.

    b. have them repeat the strategy inside their head.

    c. tell them, "Try it and you will like it."

    d. model the strategy and overtly verbalize the steps.

18. (LG 4) Which of the following is *not* a characteristic of self-regulated learners?

    a. Set goals for extending their knowledge

    b. Maintain use of one strategy in solving problems

    c. Monitor progress toward a goal

    d. Evaluate obstacles that may arise

D. CRITICAL THINKING QUESTIONS

1. A third grade teacher is concerned about one of her students' inability to understand how to subtract multiple digit numbers. On this particular day, two psychologists happen to be at her school. She asks them for assistance with her situation, unaware that one was trained in the information-processing approach and the other was trained in the cognitive development approach. Describe the advice she might get from each psychologist. (LG 1)

2. Memory is influenced by personal perspective. Consider how various customers or bystanders might remember the details of a bank robbery. Explain how their memory of this trauma might differ from other memories. (LG 2)

E. CONCEPTUAL QUESTIONS

1. What is the best way for you to study this chapter for your next text in this class? What strategies might you employ? (LG 2)

2. Imagine you are a teacher of a current events class. What specific tactics might you use to foster critical thinking in your students? (LG 3)

G. APPLICATIONS

Test a child's memory. Give them several numbers to memorize and see how they do. Start by giving them two digits, then three, then four, increasing until they reply incorrectly two times in a row. For example: Tell them these numbers and ask them to repeat them to you.

1-7

4-9-2

5-8-3-0

6-0-7-3-2

etc.

How did they do? Were their results normal for their age?

ANSWER KEY

B. TRUE OR FALSE KEY CONTENT QUESTIONS

1. T (242–243)
2. F (243)
3. T (243)
4. T (243)
5. F (245)
6. T (245)
7. F (246)
8. F (246)
9. T (247)
10. T (248)
11. T (248–249)
12. T (250–251)
13. F (252)
14. F (253)
15. T (254)
16. T (256)
17. T (257)
18. T (257–258)
19. F (260)
20. T (262)
21. F (262–263)
22. F (267)
23. T (270–271)
24. T (272–273)

C. MATCHING KEY PEOPLE QUESTIONS

1. C (247–248)
2. E (253–254)
3. D (249)
4. L (253)
5. B (253)
6. M (257)
7. F (259)
8. A (242–243)
9. G (265)
10. K (267)

D. MULTIPLE CHOICE KNOWLEDGE QUESTIONS

1. b (242–243)
2. a (243)
3. b (245)
4. a (245)
5. c (247)
6. a (248)
7. a (250–251)
8. a (252)
9. d (253–254)
10. c (254–255)
11. c (254)
12. b (256)
13. c (260)
14. c (267)
15. c (267)
16. c (270–271)
17. d (271–272)
18. b (272–273)

E. CRITICAL THINKING QUESTIONS

1. (242–243)
   - Both psychologists would try to identify the student's mental capacity. The information-processing psychologist might focus more on process. An example would be to engage in problem-solving strategies to overcome the student's lack of understanding. This might include analysis of the content and the instructional procedures: how can the concept be broken down into smaller parts?
   - The cognitive-development psychologist might focus more on cognitive products. Grounded in stage theory this psychologist would look at developmental expectations. Perhaps the student is cognitively between the preoperation stage and concrete operation stage. This student probably needs to work on classification skills before learning the mechanics of subtraction.

2. (257–259)
   - Memories of personal traumas tend to be more accurate and longer lasting than memory for an ordinary event. Thus the memory should be vivid and detailed.
   - However, memories of personal traumas may also be inaccurate because the experience was shocking, they recalled the episode as being less traumatic than it actually was, or they included others' recollections into the event.
   - If the event was particularly traumatic, a witness is at risk for developing Post-traumatic Stress Disorder.

F. CONCEPTUAL QUESTIONS

1. Some strategies you might employ include (244–257):
   - Using selective attention: focusing selectively on this chapter and not on the TV that might be playing in the background
   - Using rehearsal prior to taking the exam
   - Processing the information at a deeper level
   - Using elaboration by relating the information in the chapter to your own life
   - Trying to make the information distinct in your memory
   - Using imagery
   - Organizing the information, such as using chunking
   - Studying for this chapter last if you have other subjects for which you need to study
   - Studying close to the time of the test to prevent decay

2. Some ideas are (267–269):
   a) Describing what, how, and why current events occur
   b) Examining the facts and their supporting evidence
   c) Promoting non-emotional, logical arguments on various topics
   d) Asking new questions on the topic
   e) Looking at newspapers from other countries on the same current event topic
   f) Promoting discussion of different strategies to solve a current conflict
   g) Having students create their own newspaper stories and using "intellectual carefulness" by checking for organization and accuracy

CHAPTER 9: INTELLIGENCE

A. LEARNING GOALS

The Nature of Intelligence

LG 1: Describe What Intelligence Is.

Intelligence Testing

LG 2: Explain How Intelligence is Measured and the Limitations of Intelligence Tests.

Theories of Multiple Intelligence

LG 3: Evaluate Theories of Multiple Intelligence.

Intelligence in Infancy and Developmental Transformations

LG 4: Summarize the Testing of Intelligence in Infancy and Developmental Transformations.

The Extremes of Intelligence and Creativity

LG 5: Discuss Characteristics of Mental Retardation, Giftedness, and Creativity.

The Influence of Heredity and Environment on Intelligence

LG 6: Analyze the Contributions of Heredity and Environment to Intelligence.

B. TRUE OR FALSE KEY CONTENT QUESTIONS

The Nature of Intelligence

1. T F   Intelligence is the ability to solve problems and learn from experience. (LG 1)

Intelligence Testing

2. T F   The term intelligence quotient (IQ) is an individual's chronological age

                        divided by his/her mental age. (LG 2)

3. T F   The Stanford-Binet test is given to individuals from birth to two years old. (LG 2)

4. T F   The Weschsler Scales measure verbal, performance, and information

                        characteristics. (LG 2)

5. T F   Validity means a test measures the attribute it is suppose to measure. (LG 2)

6. T F   The consistency of a test's measure of performance is called reliability. (LG 2)

7. T F   A test that is reliable is also valid. (LG 2)

8. T F   Culture-fair tests of intelligence require time limits. (LG 2)

Theories of Multiple Intelligence

9. T F   Gardner's Multiple Intelligence theory emphasizes eight frames of mind. (LG 3)

10. T F   Robert Sternberg's Triarchic Theory argues that the basic unit of intelligence is a

                        component to process information. (LG 3)

Intelligence in Infancy & Developmental Transformations

11. T F   Due to later rapid cognitive growth there is no correlation between IQ scores of an eight

                        year old and a ten year old. (LG 4)

12. T F   Advances in information-processing assessment conclude that infant tasks

                        involving attention are closely related to later standardized intelligence

                        tests in childhood. (LG 4)

The Extremes of Intelligence and Creativity

13. T   F   An individual who is mentally retarded has an IQ below 80. (LG 5)

14. T   F   An individual who is gifted has an IQ of 120 or higher. (LG 5)

15. T   F   An individual who is creative is likely to be a convergent thinker. (LG 5)

The Influence of Heredity and Environment on Intelligence

16. T   F   Heritability refers to the fraction of the variance in IQ in a population that is

attributed to the environment. (LG 6)

C. MATCHING KEY PEOPLE QUESTIONS

___ 1. The author of a theory of intelligence that assumes eight frames of mind. (LG 3)

___ 2. The individual who encourages a child's natural curiosity and cautions adults not to overcontrol a child's creativity. (LG 5)

___ 3. The author of the triarchic theory of intelligence. (LG 3)

___ 4. The author of the two-factor theory of intelligence that assumes there is a general intelligence and a number of specific types of intelligence. (LG 3)

___ 5. The individual who developed the concept of mental age in his effort to devise a method for determining which students would not benefit from typical school instruction. (LG 2)

___ 6. The individual who developed the infant development assessment. (LG 4)

___ 7. The author of the most widely used individual intelligence test other than revised versions of the Stanford-Binet. (LG 2)

___ 8. The individual who initiated revisions of Binet's intelligence test, and longitudinal research on 1,500 gifted persons. (LG 4)

A. Alfred Binet

B. David Wechsler

C. Charles Spearman

D. L.L. Thurstone`

E. Howard Gardner

F. Robert J. Sternberg

G. Arnold Gesell

H. Nancy Bayley

I. Robert McCall

J. Lewis Terman

K. J. P. Guillford

L. Mihaly Csikszentmihalyi

M. Teresa Amabile

D. MULTIPLE CHOICE KNOWLEDGE QUESTIONS

1. (LG 1) Which of the following is *not* an aspect of intelligence?

    a. Involves ability to adapt

    b. Can be measured directly

    c. Includes individual differences and assessment

    d. Can compare the intellectual acts that people perform

2. (LG 2) Joe has a mental age of eight and a chronological age of ten. Joe's IQ is

    a. 80.

    b. 100.

    c. 125.

    d. 160.

3. (LG 2) Which is *not* an important area in the latest edition of the Standford-Binet test?

    a. verbal reasoning

    b. short-term memory

    c. perceptual speech

    d. visual reasoning

4. (LG 2) One of the main advantages of the Wechsler scales over the Binet test is that the Wechsler scales include measures that are

    a. progressive.

    b. culturally specific.

    c. not verbal.

    d. screens for brain damage.

5. (LG 2) The psychometric approach to intelligence

    a. focuses on intellectual changes that shape the organization of adolescent intelligence.

    b. ignores individual differences and emphasizes the dynamic nature of intelligence.

    c. is not concerned with predicting intelligence at a later point in development.

    d. focuses on individual differences and seeks to measure them.

6. (LG 2) _____ is the extent to which a test yields a consistent, reproducible measure of a child's performance.

    a. Standardization

    b. Reliability

    c. Concurrent validity

    d. Criterion validity

7. (LG 2) Some intelligence tests have been constructed without any verbal items in an attempt to make them

    a. more reliable.

    b. better able to predict school success in normal schools.

    c. culturally fair.

    d. better able to identify children with strong psychomotor skills.

8. (LG 3) Howard Gardner is known for

    a. his emphasis on multiple intelligences.

    b. revising the original Binet test for use in the United States.

    c. devising the formula for IQ.

    d. his arguments that intelligence consists only of verbal and mathematical abilities.

9. (LG 3) An Olympic gymnast would have a strength in which type of intelligence according to Gardner?

    a. spatial skills

    b. bodily-kinesthetic skills

    c. naturalist skills

    d   physical skills

10. (LG 3) Which of the following is an example of practical intelligence, according to Sternberg?

    a. finding a cure for a disease

    b. not falling for a phone scam promising you instant wealth

    c. graduating top in your high school class

    d. creating a new invention

11. (LG 4) Which of the following best describes the stability of intelligence via IQ tests in childhood?

    a. Intelligence is stable across the first six years of life.

    b. The strongest stability of intelligence is across the adolescent years.

    c. The strongest stability of intelligence is across ages nine and ten.

    d. Intelligence is not stable across the preadolescent and adolescent years.

12. (LG 5) The smallest numbers of mentally retarded individuals are in the category of _____ retardation.

    a. mild

    b. moderate

    c. severe

    d. profound

13. (LG 5) Which of the following forms of mental retardation is caused by the presence of an extra chromosome?

    a. Down syndrome

    b. cretinism

    c. PKU

    d. cultural-familial retardation

14. (LG 5) Gifted individuals

    a. have above-average intelligence.

    b. have a superior talent.

    c. have academic aptitude.

    d. All of the above are correct.

15. (LG 5) Producing novel responses to problems

    a. is creativity.

    b. may be the product of high intelligence.

    c. is convergent thinking.

    d. All of the above are correct.

16. (LG 5) A psychology professor asks his students to think of as many uses as possible for a paper clip. The professor is encouraging

    a. brainstorming.

    b. divergent thinking.

    c. convergent thinking.

    d. ideational originality.

17. (LG 6) Most current researchers believe

    a. intelligence is strongly genetic.

    b. intelligence has a strong genetic influence only in childhood.

    c. the environment can change IQ scores.

    d. intelligence affects individuals the same across all cultures.

18. (LG 6) Applying what you know about gender and intelligence, which of the following statements

    is most likely to be true?

    a. Sally is much more intelligent than Jeff.

    b. Jeff is much more intelligent than Sally.

    c. Sally is better with spatial reasoning than Jeff.

    d. Sally and Jeff have similar scores on an intelligence test.

E. CRITICAL THINKING QUESTIONS

1.   What is the difference between multiple intelligences and talent or ability? (LG 3)

2.   Given the limitations, why even bother to use IQ tests? (LG 2)

F. CONCEPTUAL QUESTIONS

1. Using Project Spectrum and the Key School as models, how would you design a first-grade classroom

that tapped into all of Gardner's intelligence types? (LG 3)

2. How can you stimulate creativity in children? (LG 5)

G. APPLICATIONS

Using Gardner's eight intelligence types, how would you rate yourself in each area? Which of the types did your grade school emphasize? Which of the types did your family emphasize?

ANSWER KEY

B. TRUE OR FALSE KEY CONTENT QUESTIONS

1. T (281)
2. F (282)
3. F (282–283)
4. T (282–283)
5. T (285–286)
6. T (286)
7. F (286)
8. F (287)
9. T (289–290)
10. T (291–292)
11. F (296)
12. T (297)
13. F (298)
14. F (299)
15. F (300–301)
16. F (303)

C. MATCHING KEY PEOPLE QUESTIONS

1. E (289–290)
2. M (301)
3. F (291–292)
4. C (289–290)
5. A (282)
6. H (295)
7. B (282–283)
8. J (299)

D. MULTIPLE CHOICE KNOWLEDGE QUESTIONS

1. b (281)
2. a (282)
3. c (282–283)
4. c (283–284)
5. d (285–286)
6. b (286)
7. c (287)
8. a (289–290)
9. b (289–290)
10. b (292)
11. c (296)
12. d (298)
13. a (298)
14. d (299)
15. a (301)
16. b (301)
17. c (304–305)
18. d (307)

E. CRITICAL THINKING QUESTIONS

1. (289–290)
   - Gardner characterizes intelligence as frames of the mind. These domains (verbal, math, spatial, movement, music, interpersonal, intrapersonal, and naturalistic) represent different mental domains. The theory of multiple intelligences is being applied in pilot projects in select schools. The emphasis seems to be using multiple intelligences to further skill development. However, like talent or ability, it is very difficult to measure multiple intelligences. Presently, the value of educational applications of the theory of multiple intelligence is suggestive rather than prescriptive. Much more research is needed.

2. (288)
   - Three significant challenges to standardized testing were reviewed in the text. Controversies continue in defining intelligence by heredity or environment, measuring intelligence in a culturally and ethnically fair manner, and using the results of intelligence tests appropriately. Despite these limitations, intelligence tests are still widely used. However, intelligence tests were never meant to be the only source of assessment. Intelligence tests can provide specific information about an array of mental abilities. IQ tests are most effective when used in conjunction with an individual's medical background, developmental history, and family experiences.

F. CONCEPTUAL QUESTIONS

1. Overall, your classroom might have stations that tap into different types of intelligence. One station could include interlocking blocks that can be used to stimulate spatial and mathematical skills. Another station could include musical instruments and a portable CD player where children could play a variety of instruments and listen to different types of music to promote their musical skills. A third station could include various plants and flowers that the children plant and care for themselves to promote naturalistic skills. These are just some suggestions for your classroom. (289–290)

2. The following are ways to guide children's creative thinking (300–302):
   - Have children engage in brainstorming
   - Create an environment that stimulates their creativity
   - Take children to places that value creativity such as museums
   - Let children select their interests
   - Support children's interests and refrain from hovering over them
   - Emphasize internal reward of work versus external prizes
   - Foster flexible and playful thinking
   - Introduce children to creative people

CHAPTER 10: LANGUAGE DEVELOPMENT

A. *LEARNING GOALS*

What is Language?

LG 1: Define Language and Describe Its Rule Systems.

Biological and Environmental Influences

LG 2: Discuss the Biological and Environmental Aspects of Language.

Language and Cognition

LG 3: Evaluate How Language and Cognition are Linked.

How Language Develops

LG 4: Describe How Language Develops in Children.

Bilingualism

LG 5: Summarize What Is Known about Bilingualism and Bilingual Education.

B. TRUE OR FALSE KEY CONTENT QUESTIONS

What is Language?

1. T F   Language is a system of symbols used to communicate. (LG 1)

2. T F   Syntax involves the meaning of words and sentences. (LG 1)

Biological and Environmental Influences

3. T F   Humans acquired language about 10,000 years ago. (LG 2)

4. T F   Children throughout the world develop language milestones at different times due to the

variation in language. (LG 2)

5. T F   Damage to Broca's area often causes problems in speech production, whereas damage

to Wernicke's area often causes problems in language comprehension. (LG 2)

6. T F   The critical period for language acquisition occurs between 18 months and

puberty. (LG 2)

Language and Cognition

7. T F   Children with Williams Syndrome have excellent verbal skills but low IQ. (LG 3)

8. T F   Cognition is necessary for language development. (LG 3)

How Language Develops

9. T F   A child's first words are spoken between 12 and 18 months. (LG 4)

10. T F   Children from poor economic backgrounds hear about the same number of words from

their parents as do children from middle-class economic backgrounds. (LG 4)

11. T F   Children who enter school with less verbal skill and less phonological awareness are

most at risk. (LG 4)

12. T F   The basic skills and phonics approach to reading emphasizes whole and meaningful

instruction. (LG 4)

Bilingualism

13. T   F   Critics of bilingualism argue that bilingualism interferes with the performance of both languages. (LG 5)

14. T   F   Success in learning a second language is greater in childhood than in adolescence. (LG 5)

C. MATCHING KEY PEOPLE QUESTIONS

___ 1. The individual who proposed that there is a critical period for learning language. (LG 2)

___ 2. The individual who devised mean length of utterance to measure children's language

       maturity. (LG 2)

___ 3. The individual who proposed that children are born with an innate grammatical ability that

       underlies all languages. (LG 2)

___ 4. The researcher who studied the ability of infants to understand speech sounds. (LG 4)

___ 5. The individual who identified an area of the left hemisphere of the brain that allows articulation

       and comprehension. (LG 2)

___ 6. The psychologist who developed the concept of language acquisition support

       system (LASS). (LG 2)

___ 7. Studied the relationship between income level and language acquisition. (LG 2)

A. Patricia Kuhl

B. Paul Broca

C. Noam Chomsky

D. Eric Lenneberg

E. Roger Brown

F. Naomi Baron

G. Jerome Bruner

H. Janellen Huttenlocher

I. Lois Bloom

J. Betty Hart and Todd Risley

D. MULTIPLE CHOICE KNOWLEDGE QUESTIONS

1. (LG 1) All languages share which of the following characteristics?

    a. words and sequencing

    b. infinite generativity and multiple levels of rules

    c. words and displacement

    d. meaning and structure

2. (LG 1) Phonology is the study of

    a. use of language.

    b. order of the words of a language.

    c. associations of the words of a language.

    d. sounds of a language.

3. (LG 1) How many morphemes does the word "worker" have?

    a. one

    b. two

    c. three

    d. four

4. (LG 1) The statement, "My car was hit by a speeding lamp post"

    a. is grammatically incorrect.

    b. demonstrates improper pragmatics.

    c. suffers from poor displacement.

    d. violates syntactical restrictions.

5. (LG 1) Japanese children must learn to say thank you with "arigato" in formal settings, with "domo" to a social inferior, and with "arigato gazaimasu" to a social superior. These variations reflect a _____ aspect of language.

    a. pragmatic

    b. phonetic

    c. syntactical

    d. grammatical

6. (LG 2) Chomsky's view of language argues that

    a. language is innate.

    b. language is acquired through reinforcement.

    c. language results from sensorimotor knowledge.

    d. language acquisition relies both on built-in structures and on principles of learning and cognition.

7. (LG 2) Timmy says to his father, "More milk, Daddy." The father says back to his child, "Shall I get you some more milk?" This is an example of

    a. prompting.

    b. echoing.

    c. expanding.

    d. recasting.

8. (LG 3) The finding that deaf children who have no command of written or sign language perform the same on some problem-solving tasks as peers without hearing problems supports the view that

    a. language is an important foundation for thinking.

    b. perception and experience must give rise to language functions in humans.

    c. cognition is an important foundation of language.

    d. cognition is universal; language is irrelevant to its function.

9.   (LG 4) In teaching children to read, the currently accepted method is the

   a. ABC method alone.

   b. whole-word method with the phonics method.

   c. whole-word method alone.

   d. phonics method alone.

10.   (LG 5) Which of the following is *not* a positive aspect of bilingualism?

   a. Performing better on tests of attentional control

   b. Exhibiting cognitive flexibility

   c. Having better skills at detecting errors of grammar

   d. Performing better on tests of reading

E. CRITICAL THINKING QUESTIONS

1. Discuss the challenges faced in bilingual education. (LG 5)

F. CONCEPTUAL QUESTIONS

1. Vincent is a 16-month-old toddler who does not speak much. Assuming he does not have any kind of speech disorder, what might account for his delay in speaking?   (LG 2)

2. How would you advise a schoolteacher on the best ways to promote literacy development in children? (LG 4)

G. APPLICATIONS

1. What was your first distinguishable word or words and when did you say it (them)? Was it a name of a familiar person, animal, object, or food? Think back to when you were first learning to read and write. What technique or techniques did your school use to teach you? Compare your history with the information from this chapter.

ANSWER KEY

B. TRUE OR FALSE KEY CONTENT QUESTIONS

1. T (314–315)
2. F (316)
3. F (318)
4. F (319–322)
5. T (319)
6. T (319)
7. T (324)
8. F (326)
9. F (328)
10. F (331–332)
11. T (332)
12. F (333–334)
13. F (336)
14. T (336–337)

C. MATCHING KEY PEOPLE QUESTIONS

1. D (319)
2. E (320)
3. C (319)
4. A (327)
5. B (318)
6. G (323)
7. J (323)

D. MULTIPLE CHOICE KNOWLEDGE QUESTIONS

1. b (314–315)
2. d (315)
3. b (315)
4. d (316)
5. a (316–317)
6. a (319)
7. c (322)
8. c (326)
9. b (334)
10. d (336)

E. CRITICAL THINKING QUESTIONS

1. (336–337)
    - The goal of bilingual education is to teach academic subjects in their native language concurrently with English instruction. Bilingual educators must grapple with two issues: language acquisition and basic literacy.
    - Language acquisition takes time. Verbal proficiency in a second language takes about two or three years. The standard of proficiency in the second language is just the same as the first language: 1) Am I competent enough to communicate? 2) Am I confident enough to express myself naturally?
    - Literacy, the skills to understand academic content through reading and writing, can take four or more years. Children who do not become proficient in their second language after two or three years suffer learning deficiencies in their first language.

F. CONCEPTUAL QUESTIONS

1. Vincent's language delay could be due to how his parents have talked to him. They might not have prompted him to label objects or encouraged the recasting and expansion of his language. They might have overloaded him with demands for speaking before he was ready. Vincent might not be in a rich verbal environment where conversation is encouraged in a natural way. His parents might be falling into the sexual stereotype of talking less with boys than with girls. His parents may not have used child-directed speech or talked to him as if he were an active conversational partner. (320–322)

2. A combination of the whole-language approach and the basic-skills-and-phonetics-approach would be the best way to promote literacy development. The basic-skills-and-phonetics approach is best when combined with letter training and is embedded in a whole language system. The best phonological awareness training involves the skills of blending and segmentation. Phonological awareness should also be integrated with reading and writing. Small group teaching is preferred to large group teaching. Cognitive strategies of monitoring one's reading progress and summarizing passages would also be beneficial. (334)

SECTION 4: SOCIOEMOTIONAL DEVELOPMENT

CHAPTER 11: EMOTIONAL DEVELOPMENT

A. LEARNING GOALS

Exploring Emotion

LG 1: Discuss Basic Aspects of Emotion.

Development of Emotion

LG 2: Describe the Development of Emotion.

Emotional Problems, Stress, and Coping

LG 3: Summarize the Nature of Depression, Suicide, Stress, and Coping.

Temperament

LG 4: Characterize Temperament.

Attachment

LG 5: Explain Attachment and Its Development.

B. *TRUE OR FALSE KEY CONTENT QUESTIONS*

Defining Emotion

1. T F   One characteristic of nearly all classifications of emotion are active affectivity and passive affectivity. (LG 1)

2. T F   Research indicates that emotions play a small role in whether a child's peer relations are successful or unsuccessful. (LG 1)

3. T F   As a child gets older, emotional regulation shifts from self-initiated sources to external sources. (LG 1)

Development of Emotion

4. T F   The basic cry is probably caused by hunger. (LG 2)

5. T F   Social referencing means reading emotional cues to determine how to act in a particular situation. (LG 2)

6. T F   Moodiness in early adolescence reduces an individual's chance to become a competent adult. (LG 2)

Emotional Problems, Stress, and Coping

7. T F   Seligman believes that learned helplessness, caused by prolonged exposure to negative experiences over which there is no control, leads to depression. (LG 3)

8. T F   Lazarus' cognitive appraisal is a way children interpret stress as either harmful, threatening, or challenging. (LG 3)

9. T F   Firsthand contact between two different cultural groups can cause stress. (LG 3)

Temperament

10. T F   Most parents believe in the importance of temperament with the birth of their first

child. (LG 4)

11. T F   Children's temperament can vary across cultures. (LG 4)

Attachment

12. T F   Feeding is more important than contact comfort in establishing attachment. (LG 5)

13. T F   Caregivers of secure babies are sensitive to their signals and are consistently available to

meet their needs. (LG 5)

14. T F   A mother's role to the child is largely caregiving; a father's role is largely playful

interaction. (LG 5)

15. T F   In stressful circumstances, infants often prefer their mother to their father. (LG 5)

16. T F   More than 12 million young children currently attend licensed day care. (LG 5)

17. T F   The recommended ratio of children to adult caregivers for three year olds

is 15:1. (LG 5)

18. T F   The NICHD study showed that childcare adversely affected the security of infants'

attachment to their mother. (LG 5)

C. MATCHING KEY PEOPLE QUESTIONS

___ 1. The psychologist who believed people become depressed due to acquiring a negative cognitive schema early in their development. (LG 3)

___ 2. The researcher who devised the Strange Situation to measure attachment. (LG 5)

___ 3. Identified the basic temperaments as the easy child, the difficult child, and the slow-to-warm-up child. (LG 4)

___ 4. The individual who studied nontraditional gender roles in Swedish families. (LG 5)

___ 5. The researcher who demonstrated feeding is not the crucial element in forming an attachment. (LG 5)

___ 6. The psychiatrist who believed that an infant and his or her caregiver instinctively form an attachment. (LG 5)

___ 7. The psychologist who believes emotional competence involves the developing of a number of skills. (LG 1)

___ 8. The psychologist who believes depression is learned helplessness. (LG 3)

A. Nancy Eisenberg

B. John Bowlby

C. Aaron Beck

D. Martin Seligman

E. Daniel Goleman

F. Alexander Chess and Stella Thomas

G. Harry Harlow

H. Konrad Lorenz

I. Mary Ainsworth

J. Carolyn Saarni

K. Michael Lamb

D. MULTIPLE CHOICE KNOWLEDGE QUESTIONS

1. (LG 1) Emotion is a mixture of all of the following *except*

    a. physiological arousal.

    b. cognitions.

    c. conscious experience.

    d. behavioral expression.

2. (LG 1) Parents who monitor their children's emotions and view their negative emotions as opportunities for teaching are said to be

    a. emotionally dismissing.

    b. emotional coaches.

    c. functionalist.

    d. relational judges.

3. (LG 2) Early social smiles tend to be toward

    a. food.

    b. faces.

    c. toys.

    d. random external stimuli.

4. (LG 2) Separation protest tend to peak at about

    a. 7 months

    b. 12 months

    c. 15 months

    d. 20 months

5. (LG 3) According to John Bowlby, children become depressed as a result of

      a. self-devaluing cognitive schema.

      b. exposure to prolonged uncontrollable negative experiences.

      c. insecure attachments.

      d. living with depressed parents.

6. (LG 3) African Americans living in Dubuque, Iowa who found burning crosses in their yards at night in the fall of 1991 were experiencing

      a. daily hassles.

      b. life events.

      c. frustration.

      d. acculturative stress.

7. (LG 4) A child who reacts to many aspects of unfamiliarity with initial avoidance, distress, or subdued affect has a(n) _____ temperament.

      a. secure

      b. inhibited

      c. slow-to-warm-up

      d. difficult

8. (LG 5) Erik Erikson says that the key time for attachment is within the first _____ after birth.

      a. few minutes

      b. few hours

      c. day

      d. year

9. (LG 5) Bowlby theorized a goal-corrected partnership is formed between children and caregivers at about

    a. birth to 2 months

    b. 2 to 7 months

    c. 7 to 24 months

    d. 24 months on

10. (LG 5) Mary Ainsworth says attachment security depends on

    a. how sensitive and responsive the caregiver is to infant signals.

    b. the mother's love and concern for the welfare of the child.

    c. the quantity of parental responses during the child-care routine.

    d. reinforcement of attachment behaviors by the caregiver.

11. (LG 5) Which of the following techniques describes use of the Strange Situation to investigate attachment?

    a. watching children as they are separated from and then reunited with their parents

    b. asking parents to describe how emotionally involved they are with their children

    c. watching children play with dolls representing adults and children to see what kind of interactions they create

    d. asking baby-sitters about how infants behave when their parents are gone

12. (LG 5) The major problem in assessing the impact of day care on child development lies in the

    a. wide variety of "types of day care."

    b. lack of interest in the issue.

    c. fact that so few children attend day care.

    d. lack of theoretical basis for predicting negative outcomes.

E. CRITICAL THINKING QUESTIONS

1. How can parents help their children learn to control their emotions?

F. CONCEPTUAL QUESTIONS

1. Serena is a pessimistic child who is doing poorly in math. What kind of cognitive interpretations might she be making about herself? (LG 3)

2. Noah displays the temperamental characteristics of being inhibited and fearful. What is his likely developmental course? What can his parents do to positively alter his temperament? (LG 4)

G. APPLICATIONS

Rent the movie "Steel Magnolias" and observe the variety of basic and self-conscious emotions that are displayed in the film. Also note any instances of social referencing (there is at least one) and assess the attachment relationship between the main mother-daughter characters.

ANSWER KEY

B. TRUE OR FALSE KEY CONTENT QUESTIONS

1. F (347)
2. F (348)
3. F (348–349)
4. T (350)
5. T (352–353)
6. F (354–355)
7. T (356–357)
8. T (359)
9. T (359–360)
10. F (367)
11. T (366)
12. F (369)
13. T (371–372)
14. T (373–374)
15. T (373–374)
16. F (374–375)
17. F (375)
18. F (377)

C. MATCHING KEY PEOPLE QUESTIONS

1. C (356)
2. I (370)
3. F (363–364)
4. K (373–374)
5. G (368–369)
6. B (369)
7. J (349)
8. D (356–357)

D. MULTIPLE CHOICE KNOWLEDGE QUESTIONS

1. b (346)
2. b (348)
3. b (352)
4. c (352–353)
5. c (356)
6. d (359–360)
7. b (364)
8. d (369)
9. d (370)
10. a (370)
11. a (370)
12. a (374–375)

E. CRITICAL THINKING QUESTIONS

1. (353)
   - As they get older, children gradually shift from external sources for controlling their emotions to self-initiated sources, i.e., moving from pleasing authority (or fighting authority) to learning self-control. Parents play a critical role in helping their children regulate their emotions. They can teach their children problem-solving approaches for regulating emotions, model healthy ways to deal with emotional arousal, and choose effective ways to cope with stress.
   - An *emotion-coaching* parent monitors their children's emotions and views their children's negative emotions as a "teachable moment." They assist children in naming the emotion they are experiencing and coach them on how to effectively deal with the emotion.
   - An *emotion-dismissing* parent denies or ignores their children's negative emotions. These children do not learn how to regulate their emotions and cope with stress, and have more behavioral problems.

F. CONCEPTUAL QUESTIONS

1. Serena will interpret bad events as global and unchanging. For example, she might think that she is failing math because she is "stupid" instead of thinking that more effort could produce better results. She will interpret good events as unique situations that do not generalize to other aspects of her life. For example, if she gets a good grade on a spelling quiz she will think "I got lucky" instead of having more belief in herself as a student. When she makes a primary appraisal of events related to math, she will probably rate a bad grade as (a) causing a lot of harm, (b) indicating a high degree of threat that she will fail the course for the year, and (c) resulting in a lower commitment in the future for this course. In her secondary appraisal, she will likely be unable to think of a wide range of coping strategies. (359–360)

2. If Noah's parents do not intervene, he will likely grow up to be shy and fearful as an adult because there is some evidence that temperament is stable across the lifespan. However, using the goodness of fit index, his parents can adapt to his temperamental characteristics and help him become less fearful and inhibited. If his parents use gentle discipline, he will develop a strong conscience. Sanson and Rothbart advise parents to do the following (365–367):
   a) Respect Noah's individuality by being sensitive and flexible.
   b) Provide Noah with additional support.
   c) Structure his environment by having him slowly enter new contexts.
   d) Avoid labeling him with negative temperamental descriptors.

CHAPTER 12: THE SELF AND IDENTITY

A. LEARNING GOALS

Self-Understanding

LG 1: Discuss Self-Understanding and Its Development.

global

Self-Esteem and Self-Concept

LG 2: Explain Self-Esteem and Self-Concept.

Specific domains

Identity

LG 3: Describe Identity and Its Development.

B. TRUE OR FALSE KEY CONTENT QUESTIONS

Self-Understanding

1. T~~F~~   Self-understanding is the cognitive representation of the child's self-concept. (LG 1)

2. (T) F   Infants develop a rudimentary form of self-recognition at approximately 18 months old. (LG 1)

3. T (F)   The physical and active self is characteristic of middle and late childhood. (LG 1)

4. (T) F   Contradictory self-descriptions among adolescents dramatically increase between seventh and ninth grades. (LG 1)

5. T (F)   Adolescents are less likely than children to be self-conscious and preoccupied with their self-understanding. (LG 1)

6. (T) F   Children's perspective-taking abilities can improve peer status and the quality of their friendships. (LG 1)

Self-Esteem and Self-Concept *global*

7. T (F)   Self-esteem refers to the domain-specific evaluations of the self. (LG 2)

8. (T) F   Intense physical changes of puberty are one reason self-esteem drops in adolescence. (LG 2)

*Identity
role experimentations*

Identity

9. T (F)   Two core ingredients in Erickson's theory of identity development are personality and role reversal. (LG 3)

10. T (F)   Identity formation begins with adolescence. (LG 3)

11. (T) F   James Marcia's theory identifies four identity statuses that focus on the adolescent tension between crisis and commitment. (LG 3)

12. (T) F   College juniors and seniors are more likely to be identity achieved than high school students. (LG 3)

119

13. (T) F   Both individuality and connectedness in family relations are necessary for identity development. (LG 3)

14. (T) F   Many ethnic minority adolescents have bicultural identities, identifying with both their ethnic minority culture as well as with the majority culture. (LG 3)

15. T (F)   The task for identity exploration is more complex for males than females. (LG 3)

C. MATCHING KEY PEOPLE QUESTIONS

Cooper

__H__ 1. The individual who studied the role of individuality and connectedness in the development of identity. (LG 3)

E. Erikson

__E__ 2. The first theorist to develop a comprehensive theory of identity development. (LG 3)

__F__ 3. The developmentalist who proposed that the concepts of crisis and commitment could be used to classify individuals according to four identity statuses. (LG 3) *Marcia*

__A__ 4. The researcher who developed the Self-Perception Profile for Adolescents. (LG 2) *Harter*

__J__ 5. Researchers who studied youth organizations dedicated to building a sense of ethnic pride among inner-city youth. (LG 3) *Heath / McLaughlin*

__I__ 6. The investigator who studied adolescent ethnic group identification in a predominately white American culture. (LG 3) *Phinney*

__D__ 7. A developmental theorist who studies children's perspective-taking. (LG 1) *Selman*

__B__ 8. A researcher who highlighted the importance of family processes in promoting adolescents' identity development (LG 3). *Hauser*

A. Susan Harter

B. Stuart Hauser

C. Hazel Markus

D. Robert Selman

E. Erik Erikson

F. James Marcia

G. Alan Waterman

H. Catherine Cooper

I. Jean Phinney

J. Shirley Heath & Milbrey McLaughlin

D. MULTIPLE CHOICE KNOWLEDGE QUESTIONS

1. (LG 1) After placing a dot of rouge on an infant's nose, a researcher notes that while looking in the mirror, the infant repeatedly touches her nose. The researcher is studying

   a. visual self-recognition.

   b. cognitive self-understanding.

   c. rational self-esteem.

   d. representative self-conception.

2. (LG 1) When eight-year-old Cory says, "I'm faster than most kids in my class," he is

   a. engaging in self-recognition.

   b. indicating positive affectivity.

   c. displaying identity diffusion.

   d. making a social comparison.

3. (LG 1) Over the course of adolescence, your son becomes more likely to admit inconsistencies in his behavior. This is probably due to his increasing success at

   a. achieving his ideal self.

   b. egocentrism.

   c. self-absorption.

   d. self-integration.

4. (LG 1) Children exhibiting high levels of perspective-taking have been found to

   a. have less self-esteem.

   b. interact more effectively with their peers.

   c. experience more "false" selves.

   d. have more idealistic self-understanding.

5. (LG 2) Which of the following parental characteristics is associated with self-esteem in children?

    a. expression of affection

    b. setting permissive rules

    c. conflicted family environments

    d. parental intelligence

6. (LG 2) Your daughter's self-esteem can be enhanced by

    a. having her feel good about herself.

    b. giving her praise for all of her accomplishments.

    c. giving her emotional support and approval.

    d. sheltering her from her problems.

7. (LG 3) Which of the following is *not* an example of identity as a self-portrait?

    a. A person's religious beliefs

    b. A person's academic standing

    c. A person's body image

    d. A person's interests

8. (LG 3) Kiersten is an adolescent who is struggling trying to find her identity but is not making any commitments. Marcia would say she is experiencing identity

    a. diffusion.

    b. foreclosure.

    c. moratorium.

    d. achievement.

9. (LG 3) Concerning parenting and identity development, autocratic is to foreclosure as

    a. democratic is to achievement.

    b. permissive is to foreclosure.

    c. authoritarian is to diffusion.

    d. neglecting is to connectedness.

10. (LG 3) Catherine Cooper and her colleagues have suggested that connectedness within the family has two dimensions, which are

    a. bonding and respect.

    b. crisis and commitment.

    c. self- and other-connectedness.

    d. mutuality and permeability.

E. CRITICAL THINKING QUESTIONS

1. How do the dimensions of real and ideal, true and false, and possible selves influence adolescents' socioemotional development?

F. CONCEPTUAL QUESTIONS

1. An 18-year-old college student took the Rosenberg Scale of Self-Esteem listed in Figure 12.4 of your textbook. She received a score of 18. What does this score mean? What are the ramifications of her score? (LG 2)

2. Kenny is a Caucasian American young man with an established identity. Chris, a Latino American, is the same age as Kenny and also has an established identity. How might their developmental pathways to identity achievement been different due to ethnicity? (LG 3)

G. APPLICATIONS

1. College is often the time in a person's life when they establish their identity, at least in the area of vocation. Have you discovered your identity in the areas of vocation, beliefs, and interests? If not, where would you put yourself in Marcia's classification?

B. TRUE OR FALSE KEY CONTENT QUESTIONS

1. T (385)
2. T (386)
3. F (386)
4. T (387)
5. F (388)
6. T (391)
7. F (391)
8. T (393)
9. F (396)
10. F (397)
11. T (398)
12. T (398)
13. T (400)
14. T (401)
15. F (403)

C. MATCHING KEY PEOPLE QUESTIONS

1. H (400)
2. E (395)
3. F (398)
4. A (393)
5. J (402)
6. I (401)
7. D (390–391)
8. B (401)

D. MULTIPLE CHOICE KNOWLEDGE QUESTIONS

1. a (385–386)
2. d (386)
3. d (386)
4. b (391)
5. a (393)
6. c (393)
7. b (397)
8. c (398)
9. a (400)
10. d (401)

E. CRITICAL THINKING QUESTIONS

1. (387–388)
   - Adolescents develop their self-understanding by exploring their multiple selves.
     An adolescent can distinguish between their *real self* (who they are with friends)
     and their *ideal self* (who they are on a date). An adolescent can distinguish between their *true self*
     and *false self* (who they imagine themselves to be) as well as *possible self* (who they want to
     be).
   - This differentiation helps them to see the multidimensional possibilities before them. They can
     describe themselves in terms of connections to others (family, friends, peers, etc.) as well as in
     the context of current selves (living with parents and participating in high school athletics) and
     future selves (living independently while away at college). Ironically, their ability to navigate these
     multiple worlds helps them develop the stability and integration needed for adulthood.

F. CONCEPTUAL QUESTIONS

1. This student has low self-esteem. Her low self-esteem might only be causing her temporary discomfort; but it is more likely that she is at risk for developing other problems. She might become depressed or suicidal. She has an increased chance of having an unwanted pregnancy or abusing drugs. She might also become delinquent towards school and the law. If she is also having difficulties at school or at home, her problems will be intensified. (391–393)

2. Chris had the added dimension of establishing an ethnic identity as part of his whole identity formation. He likely confronted his ethnic identity for the first time in adolescence. He might have had to deal with issues of prejudice, discrimination, or other barriers on his path towards establishing his identity. His main focus was probably on the theme of prejudice, and how the Latino cultured differed from the majority American culture. However, if he was able to establish both his ethnic identity and his overall identity, then he probably has high self-esteem. Kenny may have explored his ethnic identity but probably to a lesser degree than Chris. (401–403)

CHAPTER 13: GENDER

A. LEARNING GOALS

Influences on Gender Development

LG 1: Discuss the Main Biological, Social, and Cognitive Influences on Gender.

Gender Stereotypes, Similarities, and Differences

LG 2: Describe Gender Stereotyping, Similarities, and Differences.

Gender-Role Classification

LG 3: Identify How Gender Roles Can Be Classified.

Development Windows Of Gender Opportunity And Asymmetric Gender Socialization

LG 4: Characterize Developmental Windows of Gender Opportunity and Asymmetric Gender Socialization.

B. TRUE OR FALSE KEY CONTENT QUESTIONS

Influences on Gender Development

1. T (F) Gender role is the sense of being male or female, which most children acquire by the time they are three years old. (LG 1)

2. (T) F Sex hormones are related to some cognitive abilities. (LG 1)

3. (T) F Violent male criminals and professional football players have higher levels of testosterone than ministers do. (LG 1)

4. (T) F Freud's theory promotes the idea that anatomy is destiny. (LG 1) *

5. (T) F Children's gender orientation is due to the interaction of biological and environmental factors. (LG 1)

6. T (F) In the social roles view, women and men have ~~equal~~ *less* power and status due to gender hierarchy and sexual division of labor. (LG 1) control over fewer resources

7. (T) (F) Social cognitive theory argues that sexual attraction to parents is involved in gender development. (LG 1)

8. (T) F Girls are encouraged to be more nurturant and emotional than boys, and fathers are more likely to engage in aggressive play with sons than daughters. (LG 1)

9. (T) F Peers reinforce gender-appropriate behavior. (LG 1)

10. (T) F Elementary children show a clear preference for being with and liking same-sex peers.

11. T (F) Pressure to achieve in school is more likely put on girls than boys. (LG 1)

12. T (F) Studies reveal that nonsexist television programming such as "Freestyle" reduces stereotypical gender attitudes. (LG 1)

13. (T) F Gender schema theory suggests that a child's gender identification is guided by internal motivation to conform to sociocultural standards and stereotypes. (LG 1)

Gender Stereotypes, Similarities, and Differences

14. (T) F Gender stereotypes are widespread around the world, especially emphasizing male's power and female's nurturance. (LG 2)

15. (T) F   Physical and biological differences between males and females are substantial. (LG 2)

16. T (F)   Males are more physically aggressive and active than females, while females are more likely to focus on social relationships. (LG 2)

Gender-Role Classification

17. (T) F   In traditional gender roles, a well-adjusted male was supposed to show instrumentalist traits, and the well-adjusted female was supposed to show expressive traits. (LG 3)

18. (T) F   Androgyny education programs have been equally successful with males and females, and both children and adolescents. (LG 3)

Development Windows Of Gender Opportunity And Asymmetric Gender Socialization

19. T (F)   Girls receive gender socialization earlier and more intensely than boys do. (LG 4)

20. T (F)   The only developmental window in learning gender roles comes during the toddler years. (LG 4)

C. MATCHING KEY PEOPLE QUESTIONS

___ 1. A communication sociolinguist who has distinguished rapport talk from report talk. (LG 2)

___ 2. Researchers who concluded males have better math and visuospatial skills than females. (LG 2)

___ 3. Author of the book *Lost Boys* who discussed the influence of the "boy code" on male gender development. (LG 3)

___ 4. A developmentalist who argued that androgynous individuals are more flexible, competent, and mentally healthy than their masculine and feminine counterparts. (LG 3)

___ 5. A psychologist who stated that behavior is sex differentiated and that the differences are socially induced. (LG 2)

___ 6. A researcher who challenged the belief of cognitive differences between males and females. (LG 2)

___ 7. A psychologist who argues that the sexes are psychologically similar except in those areas requiring adaptive responses to evolutionary challenges. (LG 2)

___ 8. Stated that adolescent males must engage in socially unacceptable acts in order to appear more masculine. (LG 3)

A. Stephanie Shields

B. Sandra Bem

C. Eleanor Maccoby and Carol Jacklin

D. Myra and David Sadker

E. Joseph Pleck

F. Carol Beal

G. Janet Shibley Hyde

H. Deborah Tannen

I. David Buss

J. Alice Eagly

K. William Pollack

D. MULTIPLE CHOICE KNOWLEDGE QUESTIONS

1. (LG 1) _____ refers to a set of expectations about sex-appropriate behavior.

    a. Stereotype

    b. Gender role *how one act*

    c. Gender identity *age 3*

    d. Sexism

2. (LG 1) Which statement is most accurate?

    a. Fathers want their firstborn to be a boy, but mothers want their firstborn to be a girl.

    b. Neither fathers nor mothers express a preference regarding the sex of their firstborn child.

    c. Both fathers and mothers want their firstborn to be a boy.

    d. Fathers want their firstborn to be a girl, but mothers want their firstborn to be a boy.

3. (LG 1) On the playground, girls teach girls and boys teach boys about their gender behaviors. This has been called

    a. gender school.

    b. gender intensification.

    c. peer socialization.

    d. peer genderization.

4. (LG 1) Adolescent females watching television are likely to find

    a. fewer role models than their brothers will.

    b. accurate representations of women's roles.

    c. important lessons on managing relationships.

    d. little to identify with in terms of sexual intimacy.

5. (LG 1) Gender schema theory predicts that adolescents are drawn to sources of information that enable them to

    a. conform to stereotypes.

    b. learn about sexuality.

    c. learn about relationships.

    a. think idealistically.

6. (LG 2) Which of the following statements is true about stereotyping across cultures?

    a. Stereotyping occurs more often in less developed countries.

    b. Stereotyping occurs more often in more developed countries.

    c. Stereotyping occurs fairly equally across cultures.

    d. Stereotyping occurs more often for females, regardless of culture.

7. (LG 2) What conclusions can be made about possible gender differences in levels of academic achievement?

    a. Females are more likely to be assigned to special/remedial education classes.

    b. Males earn better grades.

    c. Females are more likely to put forth more academic effort.

    d. Males are more likely to participate in class.

8. (LG 3) According to Sandra Bem, feminine orientation may be more desirable in the context of

    a. traditional academic work.

    b. traditional work settings.

    c. nontraditional work settings.

    d. close relationships.

9. (LG 3) The view that an individual's competence should be conceptualized on a person basis instead of on the basis of masculinity, femininity, or androgyny is called

    a. gender-role androgyny.

    b. gender competence.

    c. gender-role transcendence. *(individual competence is at issue)*

    d. gender identity.

10. (LG 4) Which of the following statements is *not* true about asymmetric gender socialization?

    a. Boys receive earlier gender socialization than girls.

    b. Girls who deviate from the expected female role will receive more peer rejection than boys who deviate from the expected male role.

    c. Boys have a more difficult time learning the masculine gender role.

    d. More gender flexibility has occurred for girls than boys.

E. CRITICAL THINKING QUESTIONS

1. Identify significant social influences of gender development. (LG 1)

2. Describe the gender differences in beliefs about emotions and emotional responses. (LG 2)

F. CONCEPTUAL QUESTIONS

1. Knowing that gender bias exists in schools, what can teachers do to reduce it? (LG 1)

2. Mike is a macho adolescent who is following Pollack's notion of the "boy code". Explain what this concept means and draw connections to other information from this chapter. (LG 2, 3, and 4)

G. APPLICATIONS

Did your grade school promote gender stereotypes or gender flexibility? Did you have more male or female teachers? Visit a grade school class and observe any instances of gender stereotyping. Observe if the teacher promotes the stereotypes or promotes gender flexibility. Have schools changed since you were a student?

ANSWER KEY

B. TRUE OR FALSE KEY CONTENT QUESTIONS

1.   F (411)
2.   T (412)
3.   T (412)
4.   T (412)
5.   T (413)
6.   F (414)
7.   F (414)
8.   T (415)
9.   T (416)
10. T (416)
11. F (416–417)
12. F (418)
13. T (419)
14. T (420)
15. T (421)
16. T (423)
17. T (424–425)
18. F (425–426)
19. F (429)
20. F (429)

C. MATCHING KEY PEOPLE QUESTIONS

1.   H (422)
2.   C (422)
3.   K (425–426)
4.   B (424–425)
5.   J (423)
6.   G (422)
7.   I (424)
8.   E (426)

D. MULTIPLE CHOICE KNOWLEDGE QUESTIONS

1.   b (411)
2.   c (415)
3.   a (416)
4.   a (417–418)
5.   a (419)
6.   a (420)
7.   c (423)
8.   d (425–426)
9.   c (426)
10. b (429)

E. CRITICAL THINKING QUESTIONS

1.   (413–418)
- Deborah Tannen's research reports that girls are more relationship-oriented than are boys. In a girl's peer group intimacy is pervasive. Girls tend to take turns more often than boys when playing games.
- Boy's talk tends to be more informational. Boys tend to be more competitive when playing games. They boast of their skill and argue who is best.
- Males usually show less self-regulation of emotions than do females.

2.   (417–423)
- Parental influences—Mothers tend to nurturance and physical care; fathers engage in play; both parents emphasize conformity to existing social norms.
- Peer influences—Elementary age children prefer same sex activities; greater social mixing occurs during adolescence, but peer pressure is strong to maintain culturally-determined gender roles.
- Media—Males are depicted as more competent and powerful than are females in television programming. Females are usually shown to be sexually provocative in rock music videos. Males are more often depicted as clever, industrious, and brave, and females are shown as passive and dependent in print media and children's books.

F. CONCEPTUAL QUESTIONS

1. Teachers can create a classroom environment that includes compliance to rules, but with flexibility in certain rules to allow boys more freedom to be active and encourage girls to be more assertive. This flexibility will also allow teachers to spend equal amounts of time with boys and girls, instead of spending more time with boys. Schools can promote more male teachers in grade schools or female teachers can invite male guest speakers in to give boys models. Career women can also be invited to be good models for both boys and girls. Teachers can closely monitor the progress of both boys and girls in order to identify any possible learning disabilities in any areas without making assumptions based on gender. Teachers can call on boys and girls with equal frequency and consciously give both girls and boys adequate time to answer a question. (416–417)

2. The boy code tells boys that they should show little emotion, except for anger. Boys are socialized to act tough. They get this message from parents, peers, the media, and other socialization contexts. Parents encourage boys to have more freedom and tend to buy toys that promote aggression. Peers use the playground to reinforce gender stereotypes. The media slants programming to the masculine ideal. In general, boys receive earlier and more intense gender socialization than girls. (415–418; 425–426; 429–430)

CHAPTER 14: MORAL DEVELOPMENT

A. LEARNING GOALS

Domains of Moral Development

LG 1: Discuss Theories and Research on Moral Thought, Behavior, and Feeling.

Contexts of Moral Development

LG 2: Explain How Parents and Schools Influence Moral Development.

Prosocial and Antisocial Behavior

LG 3: Describe the Development of Altruism and Juvenile Delinquency.

Parents

Parents should be warm and support, coning
Use inductive strategies discipline and not punitive
Involuele children in family decision
Model good moral behaviour matsing
Promote and teach/children guide about
others prespectives and feelings.
Encourage serace learning
Moral education schools is provided throug a "hidden
curriculum." The moral actmopheres is prouded
through school and classroom rules.

B. TRUE OR FALSE KEY CONTENT QUESTIONS

Domains of Moral Development

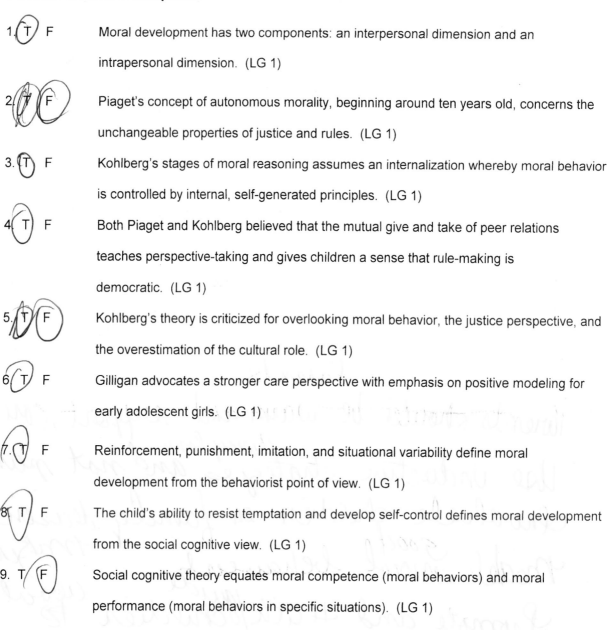

1. (T) F   Moral development has two components: an interpersonal dimension and an intrapersonal dimension. (LG 1)

2. (T) (F)   Piaget's concept of autonomous morality, beginning around ten years old, concerns the unchangeable properties of justice and rules. (LG 1)

3. (T) F   Kohlberg's stages of moral reasoning assumes an internalization whereby moral behavior is controlled by internal, self-generated principles. (LG 1)

4. (T) F   Both Piaget and Kohlberg believed that the mutual give and take of peer relations teaches perspective-taking and gives children a sense that rule-making is democratic. (LG 1)

5. (T) (F)   Kohlberg's theory is criticized for overlooking moral behavior, the justice perspective, and the overestimation of the cultural role. (LG 1)

6. (T) F   Gilligan advocates a stronger care perspective with emphasis on positive modeling for early adolescent girls. (LG 1)

7. (T) F   Reinforcement, punishment, imitation, and situational variability define moral development from the behaviorist point of view. (LG 1)

8. (T) F   The child's ability to resist temptation and develop self-control defines moral development from the social cognitive view. (LG 1)

9. T (F)   Social cognitive theory equates moral competence (moral behaviors) and moral performance (moral behaviors in specific situations). (LG 1)

10. T (F)   The contemporary perspective suggests that positive feelings, such as empathy, contribute more to children's moral development than do negative feelings, such as guilt. (LG 1)

Contexts of Moral Development

11. (T) F   According to Piaget and Kohlberg, the primary role in a child's moral development comes from peers. (LG 2)

12. (T) F   The parental discipline technique of induction, using reason and explanation of consequences, works better with elementary age children than with pre-school age children. (LG 2)

13. T (F)   The internalization of society's moral standards is more likely among lower social economic status (SES) children than among middle class SES children. (LG 2)

14. (T) F   Children's moral development advances when parents are warm and supportive, and involve children in family decision-making. (LG 2)

15. (T) F   Nearly 60 years ago, John Dewey identified the "hidden curriculum" in American schools, whereby a moral atmosphere is created through school and classroom rules. (LG 2)

16. T (F)   Values clarification is a direct instruction that teaches students a basic moral literacy that prevents doing harm to self or others. (LG 2)

17. (T) F   Among adolescents, service learning can improve grades, decrease alienation, and increase self-esteem and motivation. (LG 2)

Prosocial and Antisocial Behavior

18. (T) F   After four years old, sharing is considered an act of altruism. (LG 3)

19. T (F)   The motivation to obey adult authority figures has a large influence on children's altruism. (LG 3)

20. (T) F   Youth violence can be reduced by effective parenting and a collaborative support among families, schools, and communities. (LG 3)

C. MATCHING KEY PEOPLE QUESTIONS

___ 1. The psychologist who studied why youth kill and what can be done to prevent it. (LG 1)

___ 2. Individual whose goal is to decrease violence in adolescents. (LG 3)

___ 3. Individuals who studied 11,000 children and adolescents who were given an opportunity to lie, cheat, and steal in a variety of circumstances. (LG 1)

___ 4. The individual who advocates the use of parent induction to promote moral development of their children. (LG 2)

___ 5. The developmentalist who proposed a three-level theory of moral development: pre-conventional reasoning, conventional reasoning, and post-conventional reasoning. (LG 1)

___ 6. The psychologist who proposed a two-stage theory of moral development: heteronomous morality and autonomous morality. (LG 1)

___ 7. The individual who criticized Kohlberg's theory as being biased against women and distinguished between justice perspective and care perspective. (LG 1)

___ 8. Educational theorist who identified the hidden curriculum of the moral atmosphere of a school. (LG 2)

A. Jean Piaget

B. Lawrence Kohlberg

C. James Rest

D. Carol Gilligan

E. Hugh Hartshorne and Mark May

F. Walter Mischel

G. Rodney Hammond

H. Nancy Eisenberg and Brigett Murphy

I. Martin Hoffman

J. John Dewey

K. Gerald Patterson

L. James Garbino

D. MULTIPLE CHOICE KNOWLEDGE QUESTIONS

1. (LG 1) Jean Piaget indicates that the heteronomous thinker

    a. believes that rules can be changed because they are merely agreed-upon conventions.

    b. recognizes that punishment for wrongdoing is not inevitable.

    c. judges the goodness of behavior by focusing on the consequences of behavior.

    d. is usually a child between 10 and 12 years old.

2. (LG 1) Lawrence Kohlberg argues that the distinctions between the three levels of moral reasoning

    have to do with

    a. the degree of internalization.

    b. the immediacy of the consequences for moral actions.

    c. the severity of punishments experienced.

    d. the social pressure of peers.

3. (LG 1) Which theory distinguishes between moral competence and moral performance?

    a. psychosocial

    b. moral development

    c. cognitive social learning

    d. behavioral moral reasoning

4. (LG 1) According to psychoanalytic theory, children internalize their parents' moral standards in order

    to

    a. eliminate the distinction between moral thought and moral behavior.

    b. develop self-recognition skills.

    c. maintain a balance between parental and peer group influence.

    d. reduce anxiety and maintain parental affection.

5. (LG 1) If a person can experience another's feelings and respond in a similar way, this is called

    a. pity.

    b. empathy.

    c. sympathy.

    d. understanding.

6. (LG 2) Martin Hoffman recommends that parents promote the moral development of their children

    and adolescents through

    a. love withdrawal.

    b. power assertion.

    c. induction.

    d. altruism.

7. (LG 2) An adolescent is asked to describe his attitudes toward premarital sexual activity and then to

    think about the consequences of sexual activity and its alternatives. He is probably involved in a

    moral education program emphasizing

    a. cooperation and altruism.

    b. a bag of moral values.

    c. direct tuition of moral values.

    d. a values-clarification approach.

8. (LG 3) One of the best ways to get adolescents to volunteer in a community activity is to

    a. model volunteerism.

    b. encourage them to volunteer.

    c. have them read about community need.

    d. have public service announcements on television.

9. (LG 2) Which of the following actions is an example of altruism?

    a. sharing possessions

    b. resisting temptation

    c. saying thank you

    d. not eating food with one's fingers

10. (LG 3) Which of the following is *not* a characteristic of an at-risk-for-violence youth?

    a. Misjudges the motives and intentions of others

    b. Reacts aggressively to real or imagined slights against them

    c. Engages in frequent hostile confrontations with peers

    d. Maintains distance from everyone, including peers and family

E. CRITICAL THINKING QUESTIONS

1. Describe the predictors of youth violence and effective recommendations for reducing youth violence. (LG 3)

F. CONCEPTUAL QUESTIONS

1. Kelsie is a five-year-old child who accidentally bumped into a neighbor's table, causing four wine glasses to drop and break. How will Kelsie interpret this event according to Piaget? How will her 12-year-old brother interpret the same event, according to Piaget? (LG1)

2. Luke and Janie are expecting a baby in a month. They are concerned about raising a moral child. What advice can you give them? (LG 2)

G. APPLICATIONS

Visit the nearest hospital in your community and interview individuals who are volunteering their time to help those in need. What benefits do they experience from their volunteering? How has the experience enhanced their altruism and overall moral development? Consider finding your own "service learning" volunteer opportunity in the community.

ANSWER KEY

B. TRUE OR FALSE KEY CONTENT QUESTIONS

1. T (437)
2. F (437)
3. T (439)
4. T (442)
5. F (442–443)
6. T (444)
7. T (445)
8. T (447–448)
9. F (448)
10. F (451)
11. T (452)
12. T (452)
13. F (453)
14. T (453)
15. T (453)
16. F (454)
17. T (455)
18. T (456)
19. F (457)
20. T (460–461)

C. MATCHING KEY PEOPLE QUESTIONS

1. L (461–462)
2. G (461)
3. E (446)
4. I (452–453)
5. B (439–440)
6. A (437)
7. D (444)
8. J (453)

D. MULTIPLE CHOICE KNOWLEDGE QUESTIONS

1. c (437)
2. a (439)
3. c (447)
4. d (448)
5. b (449)
6. c (453)
7. d (454)
8. b (455)
9. a (456)
10. d (460)

E. CRITICAL THINKING QUESTIONS
1. (457–460)
  - Predictors include:
        -early involvement with drugs and alcohol
        -easy access to weapons, especially handguns
        -association with antisocial peers
        -pervasive exposure to violence in the media
  - Reduction efforts include:
        -recommit to raising children safely and effectively
        -make prevention a reality
        -give support to schools to teach interpersonal problem-solving strategies
        -create a partnership among families, schools, and community (social-
            service organizations, churches, media, etc.) that provide
            opportunities for positive development.

F. CONCEPTUAL QUESTIONS

1. Kelsie is likely to feel bad about breaking the wine glasses. She will not consider the accidental nature of the event and is likely in the heteronomous morality stage of Piaget's moral development theory. She will believe in immanent justice and expect that she will be punished immediately.
Her brother, who is in the autonomous morality phase, will not think Kelsie did anything wrong. Instead, he will consider the fact that she did not intend to break the glasses. He will probably not expect her to be punished. (437–438)

2. Luke and Janie can raise a moral child by considering the following (453–455):
  - Be warm and supportive
  - Avoid being punitive
  - Use inductive discipline
  - Provide the child will opportunities to learn about other people's perspective and feelings
  - Involve their child in family decision making, including revealing the thinking process
  - Model good moral behavior
  - Encourage service learning

SECTION 5: THE SOCIAL CONTEXTS OF DEVELOPMENT

CHAPTER 15: FAMILIES

A. LEARNING GOALS

Family Processes

LG 1: Discuss Family Processes.

Parenting

LG 2: Explain How Parenting is Linked to Children's Development.

Siblings

LG 3: Identify How Siblings Influence Children's Development.

Families and Adolescents

LG 4: Summarize the Changes in Families with Adolescents.

The Changing Family in a Changing Social World

LG 5: Characterize the Changing Family in a Changing Social World.

B. TRUE OR FALSE KEY CONTENT QUESTIONS

Family Processes

1. (T) F   Eye contact between mother and infant positively affects the child's social

competence. (LG 1) *carry over to influence develop late on it) life,*

2. T (F)   The continuity view of the developmental construction of relationships emphasizes

change and growth in relationships over time. (LG 1)

3. T (F)   Parents spend more time with their child during the middle to late childhood

years. (LG 1) *Spends less time.*

4. T F   Coregulation describes the transition period during middle to late childhood where some

control is transferred from parent to child. (LG 1)

5. T F   Parental comforting of children when they experience negative emotions is linked with

constructive anger reactions. (LG 1)

Parenting

6. T (F)   Children have fewer playmates when parents arrange peer contacts when their children

are young. (LG 2)

7. T (F)   The authoritative parenting style is restrictive and punitive and allows little verbal

exchange. (LG 2)

8. T (F)   Experts contend that child abuse is mostly caused by the individual personality

characteristics of parents. (LG 2)

Siblings

9. T F   Due to age similarities, children interact more positively with siblings than

parents. (LG 3)

10. T F   The oldest sibling is more antagonistic and more nurturant toward their younger

siblings. (LG 3)

Families and Adolescents

11. T F   A child's attachment to parents remains strong during adolescence. (LG 4)

12. T F   Moderate parent-adolescent conflict facilitates the adolescent's transition from being dependent on parents to becoming autonomous. (LG 4)

The Changing Family in a Changing Social World

13. T F   The United States has the highest percentage of single-parent families in the world; one out of four children spend part of their childhood in a stepparent family. (LG 5)

14. T F   Researchers have found that maternal employment has detrimental effects on children's development. (LG 5)

15. T F   Children in divorced families are more likely than children in nondivorced families to have academic problems. (LG 5)

C.   MATCHING KEY PEOPLE QUESTIONS

____ 1.   The developmentalist who established the concept of authoritative parenting and studied the relationship between parent responsiveness and adolescent social competence. (LG 2)

____ 2.   The developmentalist who studied children and adolescents after the divorce of their parents. (LG 5)

____ 3.   A parent educator who co-authored the book *Becoming the Parent You Want to Be: A Sourcebook of Strategies for the First Five Years*. (LG 2)

____ 4.   The individual who wrote about the effects of working mothers on the development of their children. (LG 5)

____ 5.   Authors of a study investigating hour-by-hour emotional realities lived by families with adolescents. (LG 4)

____ 6.   This individual coined the term *coregulation* to describe the gradual transfer of control from parent to child during the preadolescent years. (LG 1)

____ 7.   A child advocate who documented the problems and challenges of latchkey children. (LG 5)

____ 8.   The researcher who conducted a longitudinal study supporting the discontinuity view of relationships. (LG 1)

A.   Jean Piaget

B.   Andrew Collins

C.   Eleanor Maccoby

D.   Janis Keyser

E.   Joseph Allen

F.   Diana Baumrind

G.   Reed Larson and Marsye Richards

H.   G. Stanley Hall

I.   Lois Hoffman

J.   Joan Lipsitz

K.   E. Mavis Hetherington

L.   Laurence Steinberg and Ann Levine

D. MULTIPLE CHOICE KNOWLEDGE QUESTIONS

1. (LG 1) A child who had a secure relationship with his or her parents grows up to have many positive peer relationships. This situation is an example of

    a. continuity.

    b. discontinuity.

    c. unrealistic notions of parent-child relationships.

    d. socialization.

2. (LG 1) Compared to parents of younger children, parents of elementary school children use more

    a. physical affection.

    b. physical manipulation.

    c. routine caregiving.

    d. withholding of special privileges.

3. (LG 2) Diana Baumrind describes authoritative parents as

    a. restrictive, punitive, and allowing little verbal exchange.

    b. encouraging independence and placing limits on the actions of children and adolescents.

    c. power assertive, rejecting, unresponsive, and parent centered.

    d. undemanding, rejecting, uninvolved, and controlling.

4. (LG 2) Bill's parents have few rules for household conduct or academic expectations. They do not punish Bill when he violates rules, but merely accept his behavior. Bill is likely to develop

    a. social competence because his parents unconditionally accept him.

    b. anxiety about social comparisons and social inferiority feelings.

    c. self-reliance, social responsibility, and autonomy.

    d. little impulse control and disregard for rules.

151

5. (LG 3) Firstborn children are

    a. more achievement-oriented than those born later.

    b. less achievement-oriented than those born later.

    c. more psychologically well adjusted than those born later.

    d. on the average, less socially responsible than those born later.

6. (LG 4) Adolescents who are securely attached to their parents

    a. cannot adequately develop autonomy.

    b. show less secure attachment to peers.

    c. have more difficulty engaging with peers and separating from parents.

    d. have higher self-esteem than insecurely attached peers.

7. (LG 4) You are very depressed because you argue with your daughter about common everyday problems at least once a week, and these arguments last for more than five minutes. Experts on adolescents would tell you that

    a. this high level of conflict with your daughter will lead to later disturbances.

    b. this type of conflict is well within the normal limits, and you should not be concerned about it.

    c. if you are arguing this much now, your arguments will increase in later adolescence.

    d. these arguments will prevent your daughter from developing an autonomous identity.

8. (LG 5) After coming home from school, Jimmy must wait until six o'clock before his parents return home from work. Jimmy would best be described as a

    a. hurried child.

    b. neglected child.

    c. latchkey child.

    d. stepchild.

9. (LG 5) Research on children growing up in homosexual families indicates

    a. the children will be homosexual as adults.

    b. no differences in their adjustment and mental health compared to children in heterosexual families.

    c. negative adjustment and mental health difficulties compared to children in heterosexual families.

    d. that they will not marry or have children of their own.

10. (LG 5) Ethnic families tend to differ from White American families in that the former

    a. are smaller.

    b. show more extended kinship networks.

    c. encourage more autonomy among girls than boys.

    d. have more employed mothers.

E. CRITICAL THINKING QUESTIONS

1. Compare and contrast the direct and indirect effects of the family system on the development of the child. (LG 1)

2. What are the effects on a child if the parents differ in their parenting styles? (LG 2)

F. CONCEPTUAL QUESTIONS

1. Kyra, an infant, was removed from her biological parents due to instances of child maltreatment. Two loving parents have since adopted her and she is experiencing a happy childhood. Had Kyra stayed with her biological parents, what would her childhood and adulthood have been like? (LG 2)

2. Bruce was valedictorian for his high school. During his speech, he thanked both his mother and father for their support, with each parent helping him in their own unique way. He grew up in an upper-middle-class family and his parents were happily married. Describe what kind of support he might have received from his mother versus his father. (LG 5)

G. APPLICATIONS

What was your relationship like with your mother (or mother-figure)? What about your relationship with your father (or father-figure)? Did the relationship change during adolescence? Has it changed again now that you are in college?

ANSWER KEY

B. TRUE OR FALSE KEY CONTENT QUESTIONS

1. T (473)
2. F (474)
3. F (476)
4. T (477)
5. T (479)
6. F (480–481)
7. F (481)
8. F (484)
9. F (487)
10. T (487–488)
11. T (490)
12. T (491)
13. T (493)
14. F (494)
15. T (495)

C. MATCHING KEY PEOPLE QUESTIONS

1. F (480–481)
2. K (495)
3. D (480)
4. I (493)
5. G (491)
6. C (477)
7. J (494)
8. B (475)

D. MULTIPLE CHOICE KNOWLEDGE QUESTIONS

1. a (475)
2. d (476–477)
3. b (481)
4. d (481)
5. a (487–488)
6. d (490)
7. b (491)
8. c (494)
9. b (497)
10. b (498)

E. CRITICAL THINKING QUESTIONS

1. (474)
   - The socialization between parents and children is now viewed as a reciprocal process. For example, the dialogue between mothers and their infants is closely coordinated, like a dance. Mutual eye contact between mother and child involves high interconnection and synchronicity.
   - Children also influence parents' behavior. For example, a child's academic or athletic achievement is supported by parent participation in school activities.
   - Each family member is a participant in subgroups of a family system. For example, father and mother is one subsystem. Father and daughter is another subsystem. Daughter and other sibling(s) is yet another subsystem. These systems directly and indirectly affect each other. Lack of intimacy between a husband and wife can result in parents investing less emotion in their child's life.

2. (480–482)
   - Note the four classifications of parenting:
     a. *Authoritarian parenting* is restrictive and punitive. The parent places limits and controls on the child. This approach—my way or the highway—creates social incompetence in the child.
     b. *Authoritative parenting* encourages children to be independent. This approach —lots of verbal "give and take" amidst a warm and nurturant atmosphere— creates social competence in children.
     c. *Neglectful parenting* is a style where parents are very uninvolved in a child's life. Children from this parenting style show poor self-control and are socially incompetent.
     d. *Indulgent parenting* is a style where parents are very involved but place few demands or controls on the child. Children from this parenting style do not learn respect for others, have difficulty with self-control and are socially incompetent.

     These four parenting styles approach a tension inherent in parenting: acceptance and responsiveness on one hand, and control and limits on the other. In the family system, one parent may emphasize one role, warmth and acceptance, for example, while the other parent emphasizes another role, firm limit setting, for example.

   - Consistency is obviously necessary for a child to understand the importance of both combinations.

F. CONCEPTUAL QUESTIONS

1. Kyra would have developed poor emotion regulation, attachment problems, problems with peer relations, difficulty adapting to school, and other psychological problems. Her difficulty initiating and modulating positive and negative affect would have worsened and she would have continued to show excessive negative affect and blunted positive affect. She would have been more aggressive than non-maltreated children, and would have been at risk of developing an anxiety disorder, depression, conduct disorder, or other personality problems and delinquency. As an adult, she may have been violent towards others and, if she had her own children, may have abused them as she was abused. (484–485)

2. Bruce's mother was probably the parent who was mainly responsible for her son's upbringing. Bruce's father probably spent less time with him compared to his mother but his involvement was strong in the areas of play/companionship, social activities, and caregiving. Bruce is more empathic and has better social relationships because his father was involved in his life. (499–503)

CHAPTER 16: PEERS

A. LEARNING GOALS

Peer Relations

LG 1: Discuss Peer Relations in Childhood.

Play

LG 2: Describe Children's Play.

Friendship

LG 3: Explain Friendship.

Adolescence, Peers, and Romantic Relationships

LG 4: Characterize Peer Relations and Romantic Relationships in Adolescence.

B. TRUE OR FALSE KEY CONTENT QUESTIONS

Peer Relations

1. T F   Peer relations are especially important for children who are withdrawn and aggressive. (LG 1)

2. T F   Adolescents learn intimacy skills from close friendships with selected peers. (LG 1)

3. T F   Peer rejection positively influences a child's social confidence. (LG 1)

4. T F   Well adjusted boys are less likely to be involved in peer aggression, especially when their parents promote self-assertion. (LG 1)

5. T F   Rough and tumble play occurs more in parent-child interactions than peer relations. (LG 1)

6. T F   Peer interactions occur on a less equal basis than parent-child relations. (LG 1)

7. T F   The frequency of peer interactions, both positive and negative, increases during the preschool years. (LG 1)

8. T F   Neglected children are encouraged to attract attention from their peers in positive ways and to hold their attention by asking questions. (LG 1)

9. T F   Being belittled about looks or speech is the most frequent type of bullying. (LG 1)

Play

10. T F   Parents should discourage imaginary play in children because it diminishes cognitive development. (LG 2)

11. T F   Three year olds engage in more cooperative and associative play; five year olds engage in more solitary and parallel play. (LG 2)

12. T F   During the elementary school years, games are especially meaningful because of the presence of a challenge. (LG 2)

Friendship

13. T   F   Adolescents with superficial friendships or no friends are lonelier and more depressed than adolescents with intimate friendships. (LG 3)

14. T   F   Boys, more than girls, view friendships as opportunities to develop interpersonal relationships. (LG 3)

15. T   F   Adolescents who have older friends more often engage in delinquent behavior and early sexual behavior. (LG 3)

Adolescence, Peers, and Romantic Relationships

16. T   F   Around eleventh and twelfth grades, conformity to peers peaks, especially to their antisocial behavior. (LG 4)

17. T   F   During adolescence, peer relationships progress from same-sex groups to mixed-sex groups to mixed-sex couples. (LG 4)

18. T   F   Cyberdating is especially popular among middle school students. (LG 4)

19. T   F   On first dates, males follow a reactive dating script and females follow a proactive dating script. (LG 4)

20. T   F   The Anglo-American culture has more conservative standards regarding adolescent dating than does the Asian American culture. (LG 4)

C. MATCHING KEY PEOPLE QUESTIONS

____ 1. The individual who studied peer relations for four decades, especially how much easier school transitions are negotiated with children who have friends.

____ 2. The researcher who performed the study of children's play.

____ 3. The researcher who used naturalistic observation techniques to investigate the function of children groups and adolescent groups.

____ 4. A developmentalist who identified a five-step process about how children and adolescents decode social cues.

____ 5. A psychoanalytic theorist who believed that friendships more than parent-child relationships were fundamental to the development of adolescents.

____ 6. A researcher who described play as exciting and pleasurable because it satisfied the exploratory urge toward curiosity.

A. Anna Freud

B. Harry Stack Sullivan

C. Catherine Garvey

D. John Coie

E. Kenneth Dodge

F. Daniel Berlyne

G. Mildred Parten

H. Jean Piaget

I. Willard Hartup

J. James Coleman

K. Brad Brown and Jane Lohr

L. Dexter Dunphy

D. MULTIPLE CHOICE KNOWLEDGE QUESTIONS

1. (LG 1) The main function of the peer group is to

   a. foster love and understanding.

   b. act as a surrogate for the parents.

   c. teach the importance of friendship.

   d. teach about the world outside the family.

2. (LG 1) All of the following children will be popular with their peers *except*

   a. those who give out lots of reinforcement.

   b. those who listen carefully to what other have to say.

   c. those who try to please others even if it means compromising themselves.

   d. those who are self-confident.

3. (LG 1) Samantha has few friends at school. Other children pay little attention to her and no one invites her home. Samantha is probably a(n)

   a. rejected child.

   b. neglected child.

   c. latchkey child.

   d. controversial child.

4. (LG 2) Developmentalists characterize play as

   a. pleasurable activity.

   b. activity engaged in for its own sake.

   c. the work of children.

   d. All of the above help define play.

5. (LG 2) Mildred Parten's play categories are examples of increasingly complex and interactive

    a. models of work.

    b. social play.

    c. instructional play.

    d. games.

6. (LG 2) Practice play differs from sensorimotor play in which of the following ways?

    a. It is common in the infancy stage of development.

    b. It involves coordination of skills.

    c. It revolves around the use of symbols.

    d. It is common in adolescence.

7. (LG 3) When Bonnie informs Connie that she is afraid of boys and has never been on a date, by

    definition she is

    a. violating accepted gender norms.

    b. modeling for her parents.

    c. increasing the intimacy of the relationship.

    b. assessing the trust versus mistrust level of the relationship.

8. (LG 3) Which of the following is *not* a characteristic of early-maturing girls' friendships?

    a. Associate with girls their own age.

    b. Associate with girls who are older than they are but biologically similar.

    c. Engage in deviant acts such as getting drunk and stealing.

    d. Less likely to be educationally oriented.

9. (LG 4) Compared to children's cliques, adolescents' cliques are more likely to

    a. be made up of many types of individuals.

    b. have both male and female members.

    c. contain individuals who are not friends.

    d. be smaller.

10. (LG 4) Ethnic-minority adolescents are more likely than white students to

    a. have school friends separate from home or neighborhood friends

    b. be classified as "popular."

    c. hang around in same-sexed groups.

    d. be unconcerned about their ethnic status.

E.   CRITICAL THINKING QUESTIONS

1. How does parental or teaching style contribute to bullying behavior or "whipping boy" outcomes? (LG 1)

2. How has the function of adolescent dating changed in the last 100 years? (LG 4)

F.   CONCEPTUAL QUESTIONS

1. Olivia's favorite toy has buttons on it that cause cartoon characters to pop up, with a character corresponding to a particular button. Erich likes to build houses and cars out of his building blocks. Nikolas runs around the yard galloping on his "horse," made from a broomstick. Estimate the ages of each child mentioned above and describe their type of play. (LG 2)

2. Provide a developmental explanation for the results displayed in Figure 16.4 in the textbook. (LG 1 & 3)

G. APPLICATIONS

Observe two or more children playing together. Then, describe what type of play they engaged in, using information from this chapter. Be sure to relate your observations to the descriptions in the textbook. Did your observations match the descriptions? Think back to your own childhood and come up with examples for three of the play types.

ANSWER KEY

B. TRUE OR FALSE KEY CONTENT QUESTIONS

1. T (511)
2. T (512)
3. F (512)
4. T (512)
5. F (512)
6. F (513)
7. T (513–514)
8. T (516)
9. T (516)
10. F (518)
11. F (519–520)
12. T (520)
13. T (523)
14. F (525)
15. T (525)
16. F (527)
17. T (528)
18. T (531)
19. F (531–532)
20. F (532)

C. MATCHING KEY PEOPLE QUESTIONS

1. I (524)
2. G (519)
3. L (528)
4. E (515)
5. B (523)
6. F (520)

D. MULTIPLE CHOICE KNOWLEDGE QUESTIONS

1. d (511)
2. c (515–516)
3. b (515–516)
4. d (518–520)
5. b (520)
6. b (520)
7. c (522)
8. a (525)
9. b (527)
10. a (530)

E. CRITICAL THINKING QUESTIONS

1. (512)
    - Bullies' parents—authoritarian and rejecting of their children, yet permissive about sons' aggression.
    - Whipping boys' parents—Anxious and overprotective, taking special care to avoid aggression.
    - Well adjusted boys' parents—promoted self-assertiveness rather than aggression in mediating conflict; also encouraged their sons to be tolerant and resist peer pressure.
    Teachers who encourage more cooperative interactions have less peer isolation or aggressive peer behavior.

2. (528–531)
    - During the first half of the twentieth century, the purpose of dating was courtship for marriage.
    - Today, the purposes of dating include:
        a. recreation and enjoyment
        b. source of status and achievement
        c. a socialization process to learn how to get along with others
        d. learning about intimacy and a meaningful relationship
        e. sexual exploration and experimentation
        f. helps adolescents separate from families of origin
        g. courtship for marriage
    - Values and religious beliefs in various cultures often dictate the age that dating begins, how much freedom is allowed, the need for chaperones, and the roles of males and females. Tensions can arise in immigrant families between "new world" adolescents and "old world" parents.

F. CONCEPTUAL QUESTIONS

1. Olivia is around the age of 12 months. She is engaging in sensorimotor play where she derives pleasure from exercising her existing sensorimotor schemas. Her play has progressed to the point where she enjoys making things work and exploring cause and effect. Erich is a preschooler who is engaged in constructive play. He enjoys taking his blocks and creating projects. Finally, Nikolas is somewhere between the ages of 18 months to 5 years. Given his running around the house, he is probably a preschooler. He is engaging in pretense/symbolic play where he is taking a regular object and symbolizing it as something else. (520)

2. The overall trend from this figure is that children increase their intimacy with friends and decrease their intimate conversations with parents. As the beginning of this chapter stated, children spend more time with peers than with parents as they grow older. Peer interaction provides valuable information about the world outside of the family. Friendship provides companionship, stimulation, physical support, ego support, social comparison, and intimacy/affection. Friendship is important to overall health. Adolescents who only have superficial friendships or no close friendships at all report feeling lonelier, feeling more depressed, and having lower self-esteem than adolescents with intimate friendships. Intimate conversations allow adolescents to realize that they are not "abnormal" and allow for important emotional support. Thus, this trend is part of normal development. (510–512; 522–524)

CHAPTER 17: SCHOOLS

A. LEARNING GOALS

Exploring Children's Schooling

LG 1: Discuss Some Approaches to Children's Schooling and Changing Social Developmental Contexts in Schools.

Schools and Developmental Status

LG 2: Summarize What Schooling is Like for Children of Different Ages.

Socioeconomic Status and Ethnicity in Schools

LG 3: Describe the Roles of Socioeconomic Status and Ethnicity in Schools.

Children with Disabilities

LG 4: Characterize Children with Disabilities and Their Schooling.

Achievement

LG 5: Explain the Development of Achievement in Children.

B. TRUE OR FALSE KEY CONTENT QUESTIONS

Exploring Children's Schooling

1. T F   Advocates of the direct instruction approach argue that the constructive (cognitive and social) approach makes students passive learners. (LG 1)

2. T F   Advocates of the constructive (cognitive and social) approach argue that the direct instruction approach does not give enough attention to the content of a discipline. (LG 1)

3. T F   A constructivist theme moves instruction away from the teacher and toward the student. (LG 1)

Schools and Developmental Status

4. T F   The Montessori approach fosters individual independence and develops cognitive skills, but de-emphasizes verbal interaction with the teacher and peers. (LG 2)

5. T F   Direct teaching through large group paper-and-pencil activities is believed to be developmentally appropriate. (LG 2)

6. T F   At least 40 percent of Head Start programs and 80 percent of early childhood programs are of questionable quality. (LG 2)

7. T F   Elementary school teachers "cover the curriculum" because children need to distinguish learning by subject area. (LG 2)

8. T F   The Carnegie Corporation Report recommended restructuring middle schools to smaller "communities" in which teachers team-teach in more flexibly designed curriculum blocks and lower the student-to-counselor/teacher ratio. (LG 2)

9. T F   Over the past 40 years, high school dropout rates have increased considerably. (LG 2)

10. T F   Senior high school students may graduate without the basic skills required by employers. (LG 2)

Socioeconomic Status and Ethnicity in Schools

11. T F   Schools in low-income neighborhoods often have fewer resources, have less

experienced teachers, and are more likely to encourage rote learning rather than thinking

skills. (LG 3)

12. T F   Institutional racism permeates many schools because teachers fail to challenge children

of color to achieve. (LG 3)

Children with Disabilities

13. T F   About three times as many girls as boys are classified as having a learning

disability. (LG 4)

14. T F   The most common problem for students with a learning disability is reading. (LG 4)

15. T F   Attention deficit hyperactivity disorder (ADHD) decreases in adolescence. (LG 4)

16. T F   It is inappropriate to include children with disabilities in a mainstream classroom because

it is very costly and time consuming. (LG 4)

Achievement

17. T F   One view of extrinsic motivation emphasizes self-determination, personal choice, and

responsibility. (LG 5)

18. T F   When rewards convey information about mastery, they are more likely to promote

students' feelings of competence. (LG 5)

19. T F   Low self-efficacy students are more likely to expend effort and persist longer at a learning

task than high self-efficacy students. (LG 5)

20. T F   Asian schools and parents have a much higher expectation for their children's education

and achievement than do American schools and parents. (LG 5)

C. MATCHING KEY PEOPLE QUESTIONS

___ 1. A researcher who assessed achievement by showing individuals ambiguous pictures that were likely to stimulate achievement-related responses. (LG 5)

___ 2. An educational researcher who identified the characteristics of outstanding middle schools. (LG 2)

___ 3. An educator who believed that the team approach is the best way to educate children. (LG 3)

___ 4. An anthropologist who proposed the view that ethnic minority students are exploited in American schools. (LG 3)

___ 5. Advanced the concept of a project approach in elementary classrooms where students plan and select their activities. (LG 2)

___ 6. A physician-turned-educator who developed an approach to education emphasizing student freedom and spontaneity. (LG 2)

___ 7. A social cognitive theorist who believes that self-efficacy is a critical factor in student achievement. (LG 5)

___ 8. An educator who documented the effects of poverty on children in their inner-city neighborhoods and schools. (LG 3)

___ 9. An educational psychologist who stated that institutional racism permeates many American schools. (LG 3)

___ 10. A researcher who developed the concept of the jigsaw classroom to improve relationships among ethnically diverse students. (LG 3)

A. Maria Montessori

B. Lillian Katz and Sylvia Chard

C. Jonathan Kozol

D. John Ogbu

E. Margaret Beale Spencer

F. James Comer

G. Eliot Aronson

H. David McClelland

I. Joan Lipsitz

J. Carol Dweck

K. Albert Bandura

L. John Nicholls

D. MULTIPLE CHOICE KNOWLEDGE QUESTIONS

1. (LG 1) According to the direct-instruction approach, the main function of schools should be to

    a. provide extracurricular activities.

    b. enhance the social and emotional development of adolescents.

    c. be comprehensive and provide a multifaceted curriculum.

    d. develop an intellectually mature person by emphasizing training in basic subjects.

2. (LG 1) Schools that stress cognitive, metacognitive, motivational, and affective factors use

    a. direct-instruction teaching.

    b. learner-centered principles.

    c. Montessori methods.

    d. techniques from Project Preschool.

3. (LG 2) Project Head Start was designed to

    a. provide low-income children a chance to acquire skills that would help them succeed at school.

    b. assess the advantages and disadvantages of preschool educational programs.

    c. give parents an educational daycare center.

    d. determine the feasibility of starting formal education at an earlier age.

4. (LG 2) A trend in adolescent development that has influences the creation of middle schools is

    a. an increase in formal operational thinking among early adolescents.

    b. the need for high achievement orientation.

    c. the earlier and highly variable beginning of puberty.

    d. the fact that today's teens spend more time with peers than with parents or adults.

5. (LG 2) Joan Lipsitz said that the common thread among schools that have been successful in diminishing the trauma often associated with middle-school experience was that they all emphasized

    a. gender equity.

    b. curricular flexibility.

    c. discipline.

    d. the importance of high academic standards.

6. (LG 2) During the last 40 years, the dropout rate of American school children has

    a. increased significantly.

    b. increased slightly.

    c. decreased slightly.

    d. decreased significantly.

7. (LG 3) Which of the following is *not* an accurate view of ethnic minority students in schools?

    a. Asian-American and Latino students are more likely to be enrolled in remedial programs.

    b. Minority students are exploited by the American Educational System.

    c. African American students are more likely to be suspended from school.

    d. Well-meaning teachers fail to challenge students of color to achieve.

8. (LG 4) Jack, a second grader, has no trouble with math, science, or art, but cannot spell, read, or write. Jack is likely to be found to have a(n)

    a. vision impairment.

    b. speech disability.

    c. learning disability.

    d. attention deficit.

9. (LG 4) Recommended treatments for Attention deficit hyperactivity disorder include all of the following *except*

  a. prescription medication such as Ritalin.

  b. tutoring in academic subjects.

  c. behavioral intervention with the assistance of parents and school personnel.

  d. family therapy.

10. (LG 5) Which condition promotes intrinsic motivation?

  a. Children receive rewards for good work.

  b. Children learn that success depends on effort rather than work.

  c. Children are compared to others.

  d. All of these answers are correct.

E. CRITICAL THINKING QUESTIONS

1. Describe effective intervention strategies for learning disabled students. (LG 4)

F. CONCEPTUAL QUESTIONS

1. Using Figure 17.2 as a guide, describe a good classroom that is working on the emotional area as a curriculum goal. (LG 2)

2. Mimi is an African-American student living in a poor inner-city neighborhood. Describe what her experience at school might be like. What can be done to promote intrinsic motivation for her? (LG 3 & 5)

G. APPLICATIONS

Visit a traditional grade school classroom and a nontraditional (e.g., Montessori) classroom. How do the two classrooms compare with one another? What type of school was your grade school? What instructional strategy or strategies were used? How would you design the ideal grade school?

ANSWER KEY

B. TRUE OR FALSE KEY CONTENT QUESTIONS

1. F (541)
2. F (541)
3. T (541)
4. T (544)
5. F (545)
6. T (547–549)
7. F (549)
8. T (553)
9. F (553)
10. T (553–555)
11. T (555)
12. T (557)
13. F (560–562)
14. T (560–562)
15. F (562)
16. F (563)
17. F (565)
18. T (566)
19. F (568)
20. T (571)

C. MATCHING KEY PEOPLE QUESTIONS

1. H (565)
2. I (552)
3. F (558)
4. D (556)
5. B (550)
6. A (544)
7. K (568–569)
8. C (555)
9. E (557)
10. G (557)

D. MULTIPLE CHOICE KNOWLEDGE QUESTIONS

1. d (541)
2. b (541)
3. a (545)
4. c (551)
5. c (552)
6. d (553)
7. a (556)
8. c (559–560)
9. d (563)
10. b (565)

E. CRITICAL THINKING QUESTIONS

1.   (563)
- Most interventions focus on improving reading ability. This may include phonological awareness at the kindergarten level, assistance with handwriting and spelling, or attention to listening, concentration, and reasoning.
- Intensive instruction by a competent teacher can improve deficient reading skills in many students. However, early intervention is necessary, but is often unavailable.

F. CONCEPTUAL QUESTIONS

1. Your classroom would promote developmentally appropriate practices. You would design activities to promote interaction among the children and create a classroom atmosphere accepting of individual differences. Your teaching strategy might emphasize the children choosing from a number of activities that ask them to explore their emotions. For example, you can have children create "emotion masks," and have them place them on and act out the feeling. Children would be encouraged to help one another. (546)

2. Trina's experience is likely to be less than optimal. Most African-American students living in inner-cities go to schools that have inadequate facilities and supplies. She is probably experiencing institutional racism with her teachers placing low expectations on her achievement. To improve her intrinsic motivation, teachers should give her more responsibility to set her own goals and design her own plans to reach and monitor those goals. Overall, teachers should promote her self-determination and personal choice. (556–557; 565–566)

CHAPTER 18: CULTURE

A. LEARNING GOALS

Culture and Children's Development

LG 1: Discuss the Role of Culture in Children's Development.

Socioeconomic Status and Poverty

LG 2: Describe How Socioeconomic Status and Poverty Impact Children's Lives.

Ethnicity

LG 3: Explain How Ethnicity is Linked to Children's Development.

Technology

LG 4: Summarize the Influence of Technology on Children's Development.

B. TRUE OR FALSE KEY CONTENT QUESTIONS

Culture and Children's Development

1. T   F   The future will bring extensive contact between people from varied cultural and ethnic backgrounds. (LG 1)

2. T   F   In the twenty-first century, global interdependence is a matter of belief or choice. (LG 1)

3. T   F   The United States is an achievement-oriented and individualistic culture. (LG 1)

4. T   F   Americans have distinct rites of passage that mark the transition from adolescence to adulthood. (LG 1)

Socioeconomic Status and Poverty

5. T   F   Low-income parents are more likely to discipline children with criticism and physical punishment. (LG 2)

6. T   F   Children from low-SES backgrounds are at high risk for experiencing mental health problems. (LG 2)

7. T   F   There are twice as many American children living in poverty as any other industrial nation. (LG 2)

8. T   F   More men than women live in poverty. (LG 2)

Ethnicity

9. T   F   Research on ethnic minority groups often focus on negative and stressful factors.   (LG 3)

10. T   F   Many ethnic minority individuals continue to experience persistent forms of prejudice, discrimination, and bias. (LG 3)

11. T   F   Assimilation refers to the absorption of ethnic minority groups into the dominant group at the loss of ethnic group core values. (LG 3)

12. T   F   For many years, pluralism was thought to be the best course for American society, but assimilation is increasingly being advocated. (LG 3)

Technology

13. T F By high school graduation, American children spend more time watching television than they do in the classroom. (LG 4)

14. T F The influence of TV violence on children is influenced by children's aggressive tendencies and by their attitudes toward violence. (LG 4)

15. T F The use of technology will improve a child's ability to learn. (LG 4)

C. MATCHING KEY PEOPLE QUESTIONS

____ 1. A cross-cultural expert who described the characteristics of culture. (LG 1)

____ 2. An Asian American researcher who believes that value conflicts underlie controversies regarding

ethnic issues. (LG 3)

____ 3. An anthropologist whose study of Samoan adolescents challenged the "Storm and Stress" view

of adolescence. (LG 1)

____ 4. An American social psychologist who indicated that people in all cultures tend to be

ethnocentric. (LG 1)

____ 5. The researcher who has investigated many dimensions of the information age, such as television

and computers. (LG 4)

____ 6. The researcher who studied the conditions of poverty and stress among single mothers. (LG 2)

____ 7. The researcher who studies ways for immigrant youth to cope with life in America. (LG 3)

____ 8. Television researcher who studied "Sesame Street" programming that taught children how to use

positive social skills. (LG 4)

A. Richard Brislin

B. Donald Campbell

C. Margaret Mead

D. Vonnie McLoyd

E. Stanley Sue

F. Carola Suarez-Orozco

G. David Elkind

H. Sandra Calvert

I. Stanley Sue

J. Aimee Leifer

D. MULTIPLE CHOICE KNOWLEDGE QUESTIONS

1. (LG 1) As a Russian ice-skating judge, Sergi is supposed to remain completely unbiased. Like most individuals, however, he finds that this is virtually impossible and tends to give slightly higher scores to fellow Russians. Sergi's behavior exemplifies

    a. culturalism.

    b. pluralism.

    c. reciprocal socialization.

    d. ethnocentrism.

2. (LG 1) Margaret Mead's studies of adolescent Samoans illustrate the concept of

    a. poverty.

    b. social class.

    c. cross-cultural research.

    d. discrimination.

3. (LG 1) Rituals such as bar mitzvah and confirmation serve as _____ for the adolescent citizen of the United States.

    a. rites of passage.

    b. cultural transitions of sexuality.

    c. evidence of ethnocentrism.

    d. family traditions.

4. (LG 2) Which of the following is *not* a characteristic of one's socioeconomic status?

    a. Occupations that vary in prestige.

    b. Education that varies in quality.

    c. Different economic resources.

    d. Different levels of power to influence a community's institutions.

5. (LG 2) Working class parents place less value on socializing their youth for _____ and a higher value on _____ and responsibility.

    a. cooperation; competition

    b. self-control; obedience

    c. competition; achievement

    d. achievement; competition

6. (LG 2) The individual raised in a single-parent, female-headed household is more likely than not to be

    a. sexually active.

    b. promiscuous.

    c. in trouble with the law.

    d. poor.

7. (LG 3) Until recently, there has been little research that systematically compares the _____ of different ethnic groups.

    a. educational patterns

    b. family interactions

    c. sibling relationships

    d. strengths and weakness

8. (LG 3) Concerning the integration of ethnic groups into a culture, assimilation is to pluralism as

    a. discrimination is to prejudice.

    b. absorption is to coexistence.

    c. separate is to combined.

    d. tolerance is to intolerance.

9. (LG 4) Viewing educational television is associated with

    a.   getting higher grades.

    b.   placing a higher value on achievement.

    c.   acting less aggressively.

    d.   all of the above

10. (LG 4) Adolescents spend most of their time online participating in which of the following activities?

    a.   Search engines

    b.   E-mail

    c.   Games

    d.   Music sites

E. CRITICAL THINKING QUESTIONS

1.   Characterize the following inequalities associated with social class. (LG 2)

    •   Occupation

    •   Education

    •   Economic resources

    •   Power

2.   Describe the educational advantages and concerns of the Internet. (LG 4)

F. CONCEPTUAL QUESTIONS

1. Marissa is a single mother living in poverty. What are the likely ramifications of her situation on herself and her children? (LG 2)

2. New parents ask you for your expert advice on the effects of TV on children's development. What would you say to them? (LG 4)

G. APPLICATIONS

Watch prime time TV for a week. How much violence is depicted in the shows? How many shows glorify violence and aggressive acts against others? How many shows promote prosocial development? Of the TV shows that win Emmy awards, how many are violent versus nonviolent?

B. TRUE OR FALSE KEY CONTENT QUESTIONS

1. T (579)
2. F (580)
3. T (581)
4. F (582)
5. T (584)
6. T (585)
7. T (586)
8. F (586)
9. T (590)
10. T (591)
11. T (592)
12. F (592)
13. T (594)
14. T (595)
15. F (599)

C. MATCHING KEY PEOPLE QUESTIONS

1. A (579)
2. E (592)
3. C (580)
4. B (579)
5. H (599)
6. D (586)
7. F (588)
8. J (596)

D. MULTIPLE CHOICE KNOWLEDGE QUESTIONS

1. d (579)
2. c (581)
3. a (582)
4. b (583)
5. b (584)
6. d (586)
7. d (590–591)
8. b (592)
9. d (596–597)
10. b (597)

E. CRITICAL THINKING QUESTIONS

1. (583–586)
   - Occupation
     - Greater unemployment
     - Fewer skills needed in the marketplace
     - Unstable work history
   - Education
     - Poor school readiness—read less and watched more TV
     - Fewer resources and of poorer quality in low-income schools
     - Sporadic parent support
     - More learning-disabled students
   - Economic resources
     - High proportion of ethnic minorities live in poverty
     - High percentage of single-parent families causes strain
     - Reduced government benefits
   - Power
     - Rarely the decision makers
     - Low prestige/low self-esteem
     - Institutional prejudice
     - Poor access to technology, such as the Internet

2. (598–599)
   - Advantages
     - With large databases of information, students can gather and integrate knowledge
     - Using project-centered activities, students can engage in collaborative learning, such as survey taking or cooperative scavenger hunts
     - Students can communicate globally and inexpensively using e-mail

   - Concerns
     - Disproportionate access to high-SES students
     - Disproportionate access to white students
     - Disproportionate use by males
     - Tendency to favor drill and practice to interactive higher thinking

F. CONCEPTUAL QUESTIONS

1. The likely outcomes for Marissa and her children include (586–587):

   - Exposure to poor health conditions

   - Inadequate housing or homelessness

   - Living in a violent/unsupportive neighborhood

   - Feeling powerless

   - Limited range of alternatives

   - Lower IQs for her children

   - More internalized problems for her children

   - Feeling less competent as a parent

   - Lower ratings of positive social behavior from her children

2. Television may have positive and negative effects on children. Positive effects include the influence of prosocial and educational shows. Negative effects include the influence of violent content. TV can be deceitful by showing quick solutions to serious problems. Overall, its influence can be strong because children tend to watch a lot of TV. But other factors are also important to consider in deciding how TV impacts children's development. (594–597)

NOTES

NOTES

NOTES

NOTES

NOTES

NOTES

NOTES

NOTES

NOTES

NOTES

NOTES